Inside the
Pike Place Market

Inside the

Pike Place Market

Exploring America's
Favorite Farmers' Market

BRAIDEN REX-JOHNSON

Photography by PAUL SOUDERS

SASQUATCH BOOKS
SEATTLE

As always, my thanks and love go to Spencer Johnson, my very supportive and patient husband, partner, and recipe tester, and to Bo-Bo Johnson, our kitten of a cat.

—BR-J

Text and recipes copyright ©1999 by Braiden Rex-Johnson
Photographs copyright ©1999 by Paul Souders
Map on inside cover ©Pike Place Market Preservation and Development Authority
The Public Market Center logo is a trademark of The Pike Place Market
Preservation and Development Authority.
Pike Place Market is a trademark of The Pike Place Market Preservation
and Development Authority.

Printed in Hong Kong
Published by Sasquatch Books
Distributed in Canada by Raincoast Books, Ltd.
03 02 01 00 99   5 4 3 2 1

Cover and interior design: Karen Schober
Illustrations: John Hillmer

Library of Congress Cataloging in Publication Data
Rex-Johnson, Braiden, 1956–
        Inside the Pike Place Market : exploring America's favorite
farmers' market / Braiden Rex-Johnson ; photography by Paul Souders.
        p.   cm.
        ISBN 1-57061-176-9
        1. Cookery, American. 2. Cookery—Washington (State)—Seattle.
3. Pike Place Market (Seattle, Wash.) I. Title.
        TX715.R4385 1999
        641.5—dc21   99-20535

Note: The Market is ever-changing. Some of the individuals or businesses
described or photographed herein may have moved on since this book went to press.

Sasquatch Books
615 Second Avenue
Seattle, Washington 98104
(206) 467-4300
www.SasquatchBooks.com • books@SasquatchBooks.com

Acknowledgments

I would like to thank the following special people for their assistance and support during the writing of this book:

All the farmers, fishmongers, highstallers, craftspeople, merchants, and other Market people who shared their observations and stories—you know who you are! Also heartfelt thanks to Antonia Allegra; Pam Audette; Scott Davies; Anne Depue; Joanne De Pue; Paul Dunn; e-mail buddies far and wide, especially Eileen Mintz, Norma Rosenthal, David George Gordon, Marilyn Moore, and Jane Rubey; Marlys Erickson; Don Fry; Merlyn Goeschl; Sue and Colon Johnson; Gary Luke; Sue Gilbert Mooers; Mark Musick; Nick O'Connell; the PDA staff; Nancy Pertschuk; Gene and Julie Rex; the staff of Sasquatch Books; Karen Schober; Sharron and Robert Shinbo; Paul Souders; Linda Tiley Stark; Jennifer Stephens; "Aunt" Violet Taylor; John Turnbull; and Shelly Yapp.

—BR-J

As the saying goes, I have more people to thank than space to do it in. Like most clichés, this one contains the very essence of truth. I owe a debt of gratitude to everyone whose image appears in this book. The Pike Place Market draws camera-toting tourists from around the world. Many thanks to my friends and neighbors here for tolerating one more guy with a camera. This book would never have come to pass without Gary Luke's patient prodding and guidance. Thanks as well to Karen Schober for her editing and design skills and for pulling it all together in the end. I also wish to thank my friend and editor Mia Merendino, for treating me to Pink Door lunches under the summer sun. Fellow photographer Chuck Pefley offered advice and was nice enough not to get mad if I didn't always listen to it. I owe my friend Jodi Morrison for buying the margaritas and offering the occasional kick in the butt to get me back on track. And finally, there are my parents, Bill and Louise Souders, who opted not to pack me off to reform school even when it seemed like a pretty good idea.

—P. S.

CONTENTS

FIRST THINGS FIRST

Cold Crabs at Dawn

FEW CARS OR HUMANS BRAVE THE RAIN-SLICKED STREETS OF DOWNTOWN Seattle at four in the morning. The halogen streetlights burn bright, unnatural against the dense darkness. In the middle of the Pike Place Market's Main Arcade, Harry Calvo seems perfectly at home as he begins the day's setup at **Pure Food Fish.**

Rubber gloves rise to his elbows, and well-worn blue jeans, boxy boots, several sweatshirts, and a navy blue windbreaker protect him against the Northwest chill. Over all, a white rubber apron is emblazoned with his name and the Pure Food Fish logo. A stocky man with jet-black hair, dark skin, and a long nose, he has risen to

manager after more than thirty years of fish-mongering, a career he started after two tours of duty in Vietnam.

Today, as every day, he fluffs chipped ice with his big metal shovel and then scuttles it from large plastic bins to the yawning display trays. He hoists the whole red kings, sockeyes, and silver salmon from their cardboard packing boxes and lays them out carefully, each slightly overlapping the other. The whole Maine lobsters and the fancy cooked shrimp are next. In a few hours' time, more than two thousand pounds of fish will be ready for sale.

Overhead, handwritten signs on white butcher paper trumpet "WE PACK TO GO FOR 48 HOURS. GUARANTEED." "ALASKA DUNGENESS CRABS. FRESH. BIG, FAT, AND TASTY! NEVER FROZEN! THE BEST!"

But Harry's mind is elsewhere as the radio blares oldies from the sixties and seventies. Like an artist concentrating on a difficult canvas, he arranges the red and cream-colored Dungeness crabs over a hillside of ice one by one. He culls the creatures with holes or chips in their shells and sets aside the largest specimens. When the first two rows are lined up with military precision, he sets the plumpest, most perfect crabs on top of the rest, their claws splayed skyward in a mawkish salute. "They won't buy 'em unless they look good," he reasons in his soft, gruff voice.

Left: Morning light on the bricked streets in the Market.

Right: Dungeness crabs arranged with military precision.

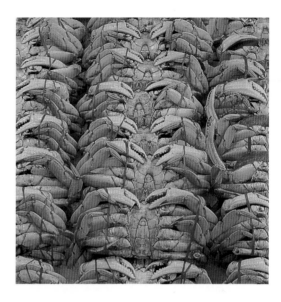

Seafood has always been a hot commodity along Pike Place, where fresh Northwest seafood changes hands with a bit of the old, hard sell mingled with a sense of artistry and showmanship. Pure Food Fish, which opened in 1917, was one of the original fish stores in the Market. Present owner Sol Amon has been in charge since 1959, when he took over from his father, Jack, who began working at Pike Place fish markets in 1911.

Like a number of immigrants who populated the Market in the early days, Jack Amon was a descendant of the Sephardic Jews who settled in the eastern Mediterranean after being driven out of Spain by Ferdinand and Isabella in 1492. Many of the Sephardim who came to Seattle at the turn of the century emigrated from the Greek island of Rhodes, south of Turkey, and from the small towns dotting the islands of the Sea of Marmara.

They poured into Seattle, drawn by the Market and the chance to work the stalls and perhaps become merchant/owners selling fish, produce, or even eyeglasses. By 1913, according to historians Alice Shorett and Murray Morgan, "Seattle's Sephardic community, which by no means threatened to overwhelm the Scandinavians or the Japanese, let alone the Anglo-Saxons, was the second or third largest in the United States."

During the 1920s and 1930s there were eleven

fish stalls within the Market, with New World names such as American Fish, State Fish Market, and Olympia Fish and Oyster Company. They were small and compact, tucked into every level and area of the old Market, and often shared space with grocery stores and butter and egg shops. Employees with surnames of Calderon, Bensussen, Ovadia, Cohen, Amon, and Levy were common. Their descendants, men like Cookie Cohen, Sol and Irving Amon, and Harry Calvo, remain in the Market to this day.

Good Morning, Raspberries

Ben Craft makes a final check of the bins of potatoes, flats of berries, and bunches of basil in his pickup truck before beginning another three-hour haul from **Alm Hill Gardens** to the Market. He and his wife, Gretchen Hoyt, have been farming their land in Washington near the Canadian border for twenty-five years and have sold along Pike Place for twenty-three. Starting out with just one acre of raspberries that produced fruit six weeks a year, Gretchen and Ben's farm business has since expanded to almost year-round production with the addition of new crops and farm-made products.

It isn't an easy life. Farmers who sell at Pike Place pick their crops late at night or early in the morning, drive to the Market for check-in by

eight, sell until five or six, and then pack up for the night and drive home. The routine is repeated throughout the growing season. Nevertheless, they come from all over Washington State, and sometimes from surrounding states like Oregon and California, with more than four hundred different products, including apples, red raspberries, and cherries—all crops for which Washington State leads the nation in production.

The farmers may sell only locally grown produce they've nurtured on their farms. They sell their produce on the day tables (also called daystalls, farm tables, or farmers' stalls), the low metal tables in the Main and North Arcades that are rented by the day to farmers and craftspeople. When you shop at the Market, you have the opportunity to become part of its age-old "meet the producer" tradition by buying and learning directly from the producer—the craftsperson or farmer.

Ben and Gretchen sell a full line of fresh produce, plus tulips, herb vinegars, and berry jams. But like all of the farmers along Pike Place, they have seen the demand for flowers, berries, and value-added products grow, while sales of fresh vegetables have fallen. It's a sign of the times as upscale grocery stores muscle in on the Market's unique offerings.

Ben continues to come to Pike Place because farming runs in his blood. His grandfather was a

Left: A craftsperson trundles a cart full of wares through the brick-lined streets.

CHERRY-ALMOND OAT CRISPS

Light and lacy when they come out of the oven, these oaty, fruit-filled cookies turn crisp as they cool. They hold up to dunking in a cup of tea or a glass of cold milk before bedtime, and they also freeze well for later temptation.

1 cup fresh tart or sweet cherries or ¾ cup dried tart or sweet cherries

¾ cup sugar

⅓ cup unsalted butter, at room temperature

⅓ cup light corn syrup

2 egg whites, lightly beaten

½ teaspoon almond extract

½ teaspoon vanilla extract

2¼ cups quick-cooking or old-fashioned oats

1 cup all-purpose flour

½ teaspoon baking soda

3 tablespoons sliced almonds

1. Preheat oven to 350°F. Lightly oil two 11 by 17-inch baking sheets or spray with nonstick cooking spray. To prepare cherries, rinse, pat dry, pit, and cut in half, then pat exposed surfaces very dry. If using dried cherries, cover with hot water until plump, drain, and pat very dry.

2. In a large mixing bowl, with an electric mixer, beat together the sugar, butter, and corn syrup at low speed until well blended and light in color. Add the egg whites, almond extract, and vanilla extract and beat at medium speed 3 minutes, or until well blended and fluffy. In a medium mixing bowl, stir together the oats, flour, and baking soda. With the mixer at low speed, add the dry mixture to the wet mixture in thirds, blending well after each addition. Mixture will be stiff. With a wooden or metal spoon, stir in the almonds and cherries.

3. Drop scant ¼ cups of dough onto the baking sheets and press into 3-inch circles. An ice cream scoop sprayed with nonstick spray works well for this. Make 6 cookies per baking sheet. Bake 14 to 16 minutes, or until light golden. Place cookie sheets on a rack and cool for 1 minute, then remove cookies from baking sheets and transfer to racks to cool completely. Store cookies in a tightly covered container, or wrap well and freeze for later use.

Makes 12 cookies

rancher and his father a dairy farmer, and it's the only career he's ever known. "I like being outside, watching the seasons change, smelling fresh-plowed dirt, and being able to complain about the weather," says Ben, a forty-something man with thick glasses and a gapped grin.

Gretchen says simply, "It's worth the trip. The Market is as much a part of our lives as we are a part of it."

In the Beginning

The idea for a public market in the heart of Seattle germinated as early as 1896, when the Seattle City Council passed an ordinance stating that *some* area within the city should be designated as a public market. But these plans became lost in the shuffle when, at the turn of the century, the gold rush in the Klondike turned Seattle into a busy port of call for those with dreams of seeking their fortunes in the Northwest.

Frank Goodwin was such a dreamer. One of seven brothers born to a Scottish farm family

Right: A new wave of younger farmers is enriching the Market fabric—often with organic produce.

near Chicago, Frank made and lost money in real estate in the other Washington (D.C.) and left there in 1897, bound for Seattle. When several of his moneymaking schemes didn't pan out, he and his brothers Ervin and John moved to Dawson, Alaska, staked a claim, and struck it rich. The trio returned with $50,000 worth of gold dust and nuggets lining their pockets and set their sights on becoming even wealthier in their newly adopted hometown.

Seattle was expanding northward along the waterfront from Pioneer Square. The western bluff formed by the steep cliff leading to the mudflats of Elliott Bay (the "under the clock" area in the modern-day Market) formed the northwest flank of the city. Rooming houses for prospectors, sailors, and other itinerant souls perched on the bluff. A rooming house called the Leland Hotel was one of the first properties the Goodwin brothers bought, along with the rest of the undeveloped mud hillside.

The idea for a public market in downtown Seattle was resurrected in 1907, when the cost of food skyrocketed due to the cumbersome method of food distribution. In those days, some three thousand small family farms were scattered throughout rural King County; down through the Black, White, Cedar, and Duwamish River valleys; and along the shores of Puget Sound. There were even more if you counted

Left: The Market is an oasis of produce and flowers in the middle of downtown Seattle.

farms on neighboring islands such as Vashon and Whidbey, which were linked to Seattle by small steamships called the Mosquito Fleet.

Farmers hauled everything from fruits and vegetables to meat, milk, and eggs in horse-drawn wagons. Some sold directly to hotels and restaurants; a few brave souls went door to door

Like well-choreographed dancers, the three Chinese bakers at **Mee Sum Pastries** work in perfect harmony in the confines of the small open-air bakery, chopping barbecued pork into slivers with large cleavers, encasing the meat in silken balls of yeasty dough, and baking neatly aligned rows of pale *humbow* until golden. The traditional Chinese buns come in several flavors—chicken, vegetable, and pork. Moon cakes, shrimp chips, and almond cookies are other temptations. According to *Chef Chu's Distinctive Cuisine of China,* "In China, street vendors sell many of these snacks in the early morning to be pur-chased by people as they hurry off to work. The vendors seem to disappear in the mid-day and reappear in the evening, again, with snacks for nibbling as one strolls in the street or park or socializes with friends." At the Market, these treats are available all day long.

hawking their goods in the city's neighborhoods. But most farmers were too busy to market their fruits and vegetables, and instead took their produce to the crowded warehouses in the Commission District, at the foot of modern-day Western Avenue and Marion Street.

The Commission District was home to the city's food wholesalers, who paid the farmers little or nothing and then sold the produce to local grocers at inflated prices. The public's outrage with the wholesalers' rising prices peaked between the summers of 1906 and 1907, when cherries rose from 6 to 10 cents a pound, and a pound of onions increased from 10 cents to a dollar.

In a populist effort to ease the cost of produce, city councilman Thomas P. Revelle proposed designating the level area in front of the Goodwin brothers' Leland Hotel as a "Public Market Space." Revelle, commonly known as the "Father of the Pike Place Market," envisioned the dirt roadway that connected Front Street (modern-day First Avenue) to West Street (modern-day Western Avenue) as a temporary site where farmers could park their wagons and sell their goods directly to families, avoiding the control of the Commission District middlemen.

When the Seattle City Council passed Revelle's ordinance in early August 1907, Frank, Ervin, and John must have jumped for joy. Whether they were the shrewdest businessmen in Seattle or simply the luckiest sons of guns in the Wild West, the Goodwin brothers realized that if the Market proved popular, their hillside investment could pay off big time. On opening day—August 17, 1907—everybody crossed their fingers and held their collective breath, for the new Public Market was nothing more than an experiment; nobody knew how it would all turn out.

Hail to the Highstalls

Alan Stott, manager of **Sosio's Produce,** is one of the first highstallers to arrive in the Market every morning around six. Highstallers are independent produce sellers who import their goods from all over the world and also sell local produce in season. Their large, permanent fruit and vegetable stands stay in the Market all year and do not move around. They provide fresh produce even during the winter months when few local farmers bring in crops.

Highstallers are similar to greengrocers, and their displays are often more elaborate than those of the farmers. Because their tables are built up higher than the farm tables and they sell tropical fruits not grown locally, a good rule of thumb is that if you can look a banana or pineapple in the eye, you know you're at a highstall.

Alan, a tall man with thinning brown hair and a mustache, unlocks the wire-mesh screen

Right: The manager of Frank's Quality Produce readies his displays at the popular highstall.

protecting the produce stand. He pushes it back to reveal green wooden bins piled high with apples, oranges, tomatoes, pears, potatoes, onions, dried fruit, and other items that can sit out overnight safely without refrigeration. The produce in these bins will turn about every three days before it needs to be replenished.

People in search of newspapers from far-flung corners of the world—Bosnia, Thailand, Egypt—head for **Read All About It Newsstand**. With more than two thousand magazines and newspapers on the most far-ranging of topics and the best selection of foreign and domestic newspapers north of San Francisco and west of New York City, the busy newsstand is a magnet for news-hungry types.

Read All About It started at the corner of First and Pike in 1979, when Seby Nahmias (who began selling newspapers in the Market in 1941) formed a partnership with Lee Lauckhart and expanded the business to include magazines. Steve Dunnington joined the partnership in 1980 and now owns two other newsstands in the city. Lee only half jokes when he says, "We cram the most stuff in the smallest space." The newsstand is open from 7 A.M. to 7 P.M., seven days a week.

On the left side of the stall—the wet side—display cases lie empty, waiting for the delicate lettuces, mushrooms, asparagus, berries, and winter greens to be unpacked from the nether-world of the walk-in cooler. Alan sets about the morning's tasks in a familiar routine, wheeling the wooden bins into their proper places, setting out the carrots and green onions, using a hand truck to move around boxes of produce. By eight o'clock the highstall will be completely set up and open for that early customer, roaming local chef, or occasional tourist in search of the per-fect peach or pear to munch on.

Just above the wet side of the stall, a charcoal mural of an elderly man surrounded by boxes of fruits and vegetables looks down from on high. The man is Sosio Manzo, patriarch of a long-established family of Market highstallers. The Manzo clan has been an important part of the Market since 1909, when Sosio, a twenty-year-old immigrant from Italy, bought a farm in South Park, just south of Seattle, and began sell-ing produce on the farm tables. Sosio and his wife had five children, two of them sons. Dan and Fred Manzo grew up in the Market culture, and in 1948, Dan gave up farming to set up a highstall. His stand, Manzo Brothers Produce, still operates a bit south of Sosio's.

One of Dan's sons, Dan Jr., and his wife, Sue, run Sosio's, so when you shop the highstalls in

Right: Corner Produce and the Market's nine other highstalls sell locally grown fruits and vegetables as well as produce from other regions and around the world.

the Main Arcade, you have a better-than-average chance of buying produce from the Manzo family somewhere along the line. The Manzos know their produce, and it shows. They are largely responsible for the brilliantly arrayed fruits and carefully aligned vegetables that help create that special Market atmosphere.

Some highstalls invite you inside to sniff the melons, pinch the peaches, and choose your own fruits and vegetables without getting reprimanded.

Don't assume that the highstalls all carry similar items or the same old stuff you can find at the grocery store. Each has its specialties. Sosio's has the Market's best selection of Northwest mushrooms and baby vegetables and some of the more unusual fruits, such as star fruit, cactus pears, guava, and French morning melons. Heirloom tomatoes are another of its specialities.

Lina's Produce and **MaiChoy Produce** feature Asian vegetables, such as Chinese long beans, bitter melon, and Thai eggplants. **Mario and Luigi's** has fruits and vegetables that are ready to eat now at bargain prices. **Jordan Village Farms** sells only organically grown produce and fresh-squeezed juice. **Choi's** features several value-added products, such as stir-fry and braising mixes. Savvy shoppers learn the distinctions among the highstalls, both in produce and expected etiquette, when they shop them regularly and get to know the merchants and their inventory.

Others have elaborate displays and signs that warn, "PLEEZA NO SQUEEZA" or "AVALANCHE WARNING. PLEASE ASK FOR ASSISTANCE." The clerks at these highstalls will pick out the products you want from boxes and bins behind the counter. Some items are priced by the pound, some are sold individually, and others are bargain deals, like "six for a dollar."

Breakfast of Champions

The hash browns are frying, the oatmeal is bubbling, the toast is flying, and several regular customers are greeting the day at the **Athenian**. Dora Otto, 72, holds forth as head waitress and maitre d', inviting customers to take any clean table they like, then proffering bottomless cups

HAZELNUT ESPRESSO TORTE

This recipe is dedicated to Seattle's love affair with coffee, a flavor that pairs perfectly with Northwest hazelnuts.

2 cups sifted all-purpose flour

1 cup sugar

1½ teaspoons baking powder

½ teaspoon baking soda

Pinch salt

2 large eggs, beaten until frothy

½ cup prepared espresso or instant espresso powder, reconstituted according to package instructions

⅓ cup canola or vegetable oil

½ cup toasted hazelnuts, coarsely chopped (see note)

¼ cup coffee-flavored liqueur

2 tablespoons grated semisweet chocolate (optional)

1. Preheat oven to 350°F. Generously grease and flour a 9-inch round cake pan. Line bottom of pan with waxed paper, and grease and flour again.

2. Combine flour, sugar, baking powder, baking soda, and salt in a large mixing bowl. Make a well in the center, add eggs, and stir just until crumbly. Combine espresso and oil, and add one-third of the liquid at a time, beating after each addition. Add hazelnuts, blend well, and pour batter into cake pan.

3. Place cake in center of oven and bake 30 to 35 minutes, or until the cake has pulled away from the sides of the pan and the middle is springy-firm to the touch. Cool on a rack for 10 minutes, then loosen edges and turn cake out of the pan. Remove waxed paper and allow cake to cool completely.

4. With a long, serrated knife, cut cake horizontally into two even layers. Brush half of the coffee liqueur evenly over the bottom layer, then frost it with half of the Coffee Cream Icing. Place the remaining layer on top, brush with the remaining liqueur, and frost the top of the cake only, allowing excess icing to dribble down the sides.

5. To serve, cut cake into even slices. If desired, sprinkle a bit of grated chocolate over each slice.

Serves 6 to 8

Note: To toast hazelnuts, place nuts in a small skillet over medium heat. Cook 5 to 7 minutes, or until nuts are aromatic, shaking pan occasionally. Watch closely so nuts do not burn. Remove nuts from heat. When cool enough to handle, rub off skins with a clean kitchen towel.

Pike Place is named after John Pike, a member of the original Bethel Party, who arrived in Seattle in 1858 and was one of the city's founding fathers. A builder and architect, he designed the University of Washington's first campus in downtown Seattle.

COFFEE CREAM ICING

1 cup mascarpone cheese
3 tablespoons firmly packed dark brown sugar
2 teaspoons instant espresso powder

2 teaspoons vanilla extract
2 to 3 tablespoons milk

In a small mixing bowl, combine the mascarpone cheese, brown sugar, espresso powder, and vanilla until smooth. Add 2 tablespoons of the milk and stir well. If necessary, add the remaining 1 tablespoon of milk and stir until icing reaches a thick yet spreadable consistency.

Makes 1½ cups

of thin coffee, the kind that Seattle and the rest of the country used to prefer before the specialty coffee craze took hold.

The breakfast menu is long and varied. Rice pudding with raisins, oyster Hangtown Fry topped with a rasher of bacon, broiled Scottish kippers, puff pastry stuffed with sauced crab or shrimp, corned beef hash, and even Philadelphia scrapple make the list. Rest assured, as you cross the worn terrazzo floor, that you will find no kiwi fruit or cilantro here.

This Market fixture has been around since 1909, when three Greek brothers opened the space as a bakery, luncheonette, and candy store with sweets made on the premises. Its central location on the Main Arcade and nonstop views of Elliott Bay helped the popular Athenian

quickly grow into a tavern, after it was granted one of Seattle's first liquor licenses for beer and wine in 1933. Finally, it evolved into a restaurant and was owned by descendants of the three Greek brothers until 1964.

You can come as you are and sit at a table, a booth, or the red vinyl stools at the front counter for a hefty dose of working-class, old Seattle charm. Everyone from businessmen to tourists to First Avenue street people stops by for breakfast, lunch, early dinner, a snack, or a drink from 6:30 A.M. to 7:00 P.M. Monday through Saturday. Actors Tom Hanks and Rob Reiner even discussed the finer points of modern dating here, in the movie *Sleepless in Seattle.* As the crowds spill out the door and down the Main Arcade, their faces are lighted by a bright neon

sign. It's the original one placed there by those three Greek brothers in 1933.

Certifiably Kosher

Michel Chriqui bustles about his small deli along First Avenue, making chicken stock for the first of four batches of matzo ball soup he will serve throughout the day. As the only certified Glatt Kosher deli in downtown Seattle, **Kosher Delight** has earned the highest approval rating from the kosher inspector, or *mashgiach.*

From the moment Michel opens until closing time each night, he knows that the *mashgiach* can come in unannounced to make certain that the exacting standards of cleanliness, freshness, and preparation prescribed by Jewish biblical laws are enforced. Inspections normally occur two or three times a week, when the *mashgiach* spends a few minutes checking the freezer for order and cleanliness, and then makes sure that the staples of Michel's business—the bread, oil, meats, and spices—are certified kosher.

Despite all the rules he must comply with to stay in business, Michel is a surprisingly happy-go-lucky man with a yarmulke perched precariously on the back of his head, an ample waistline, and sparkling eyes. Born in Morocco and raised in Marseilles, he spent many years in Israel and immigrated to the United States in 1981.

Michel doesn't see the rules and inspections as a nuisance; rather, he feels the strictures of his religion are good for him. "People respect the kosher inspector, and if he says my food is good, people will come."

And come they do. Kosher Delight was a long-established business before Chriqui bought it in 1995, a haven not only to Orthodox Jews and Muslims from around the world, but to a whole new audience of health-conscious consumers—many vegetarian—who associate kosher products with wholesomeness and quality.

They stop by throughout the day for a bite of tradition: a vegetable or potato knish, a corned beef or pastrami sandwich, potato salad and hummus, a slice of halvah or a brownie, and, of course, that matzo ball soup, all served with a smile and some solicitous repartee.

Very French

A strong café au lait and a freshly baked croissant or *palmier* at **Le Panier, Very French Bakery** is a great way to start a day in the Market. Grab a stool at the front counter and watch the Market come to life as the farmers begin setting up for the day, the artisans and craftspeople trundle their goods through the brick-lined streets, and the street musicians tune their instruments.

Left: Thierry Mougin arrives at five each morning to begin making freshly baked bread and pastries at Le Panier, Very French Bakery.

Le Panier has been in the Market since 1983. Thierry Mougin, the prototypical French baker, gets in at five each morning to begin making the store's popular baguettes and Parisians—the familiar long loaves of crusty, classic bread that many Market lovers make a daily pilgrimage to buy. Others seek out *oignon* (flavored with Walla Walla sweet onions) or *pain noix* (a rye-based loaf studded with walnuts), two specialty breads that Le Panier introduced to Seattle.

For those with a sweet tooth, a sensuous treat called the *amandine*—fresh, homemade almond paste inside a twice-baked croissant topped with fresh almond paste and sliced almonds—is Thierry's specialty. *Feuilletés* are fist-sized puff pastry purses filled with chicken, cheese, tomato, spinach, broccoli, or apple. They literally ooze butter. A *friand* is a scallop-shaped, almond-flavored

cookie. *Tarte aux poires* (pear tart), *éclair au chocolat*, mousse cups, *gâteau au chocolat*, and *charlotte au citron* (lemon tart) are other possibilities. Ooh-la-la.

The Fine Art of the Flower

Many of the Southeast Asian immigrants to arrive in the Northwest during the 1970s were members of the Hmong (pronounced "mong") hill tribe people of Laos, whose ancestors originated in southwestern China more than 4,300 years ago. The nomadic tribe, whose name translates as "free people," migrated throughout Asia in search of farmland before ultimately settling in the rural hill country of Laos.

Even in such isolated surroundings, their existence was marred by conflict, most recently as a result of the Vietnam War. Many Hmong, particularly those who sympathized with the United States, were forced to flee with little notice, carrying only a few treasured belongings. As farmers rather than urban dwellers in their home country, they arrived in the United States with no formal education, no reading or writing skills in any language, and no formal employment experience. Despite such handicaps, many Hmong wanted to resume farming in their adopted homeland.

In the 1980s, King County began the Indochinese Farm Project, a program designed

Right: Flower farmers with their made-to-order bouquets add a touch of color and beauty to the North Arcade.

to help refugee farmers get a start in this country. Located on a parcel of land a stone's throw from the Chateau Ste. Michelle Winery in Woodinville, the project has seen forty families, mostly Hmong, farm the land since its inception. Many of its graduates and their large extended families have gone on to establish a network of small farms throughout the Seattle area.

The Indochinese farmers played a major part in revitalizing the Market after the difficult renovation period from 1976 to 1980. They became consummate flower growers, and today about a third of the Market's one-hundred-plus farmers are Lao Highland families who sell year-round. Besides flowers, the Asian farmers sell what they refer to as "American vegetables" and vegetables native to their homeland, including bok choy, *gai lan* (Chinese broccoli), Thai basil, snow peas, bitter melon, and kohlrabi.

They arrive each morning before seven, their vans and pickups weaving through the throngs of delivery trucks from the city's large wholesale food businesses—Charlie's Produce, Rosella's, Gai's Breads. They pull into the few available spots along Pike Place or double-park while unloading.

Left: Many flower farmers are recent immigrants from Asia.

NORTHWEST NIÇOISE SALAD

No fish symbolizes the Northwest as perfectly as the Pacific salmon, and no salad is more prototypically French than the salade niçoise, composed of tuna, green beans, potatoes, salad greens, and vinaigrette. The two classics merge merrily when Northwest salmon and roasted vegetables of the season are substituted.

1 pound small new potatoes (1 to 1½ inches in diameter), scrubbed and cut in half

½ pound asparagus or sugar snap peas, rinsed, patted dry, and trimmed

½ pound baby carrots, peeled

3 tablespoons extra-virgin olive oil

2 tablespoons balsamic vinegar

Kosher or sea salt and freshly ground black pepper

2 cups water

½ cup dry white wine

1 tablespoon dried tarragon, crumbled

1½ pounds salmon fillets, rinsed, patted dry, bones removed, and cut into 4 pieces (6 ounces each)

1½ teaspoons Dijon mustard

1 tablespoon regular, lowfat, or nonfat mayonnaise

½ pound mixed salad greens, rinsed and well dried

1. Preheat oven to 475°F. To roast vegetables, lightly oil a baking sheet and arrange potatoes, asparagus or peas, and carrots in a single layer without crowding. Drizzle vegetables with 1 tablespoon of the olive oil, then 1 tablespoon of the balsamic vinegar. Sprinkle with salt and pepper and roast for 12 to 15 minutes, or until vegetables are tender and slightly charred, turning vegetables once or twice during cooking. Remove from oven and allow vegetables to cool on baking sheet.

2. To poach fish, bring water, wine, and tarragon to a boil in a skillet large enough to hold salmon without crowding. Remove from heat, add salmon fillets skin side down, reduce heat to low, and return skillet to heat. Partially cover (put lid on skillet slightly askew so that steam can escape), and simmer very gently 8 to 10 minutes per inch of thickness, or until salmon just turns opaque. Adjust heat if water simmers too fast or too slow. Do not allow water to boil. Remove fillets from skillet and place on several layers of paper towels or a clean kitchen towel to drain well. When cool enough to handle, remove skin and any remaining pinbones.

3. Just before serving, place the remaining 2 tablespoons olive oil, the remaining 1 tablespoon balsamic vinegar, and the mustard and mayonnaise in a large mixing bowl and whisk to blend. Season to taste with salt and pepper. Add salad greens to bowl and toss gently.

4. To serve, place dressed greens in the center of individual plates and place a salmon fillet in the middle of each bed of greens. Arrange roasted potatoes, asparagus, and carrots around edges of plates in a pleasing pattern.

Serves 4

Their stalls dominate the North Arcade. As they unload plastic buckets crammed with Teddy Bear sunflowers, delicate snapdragons, softball-sized dahlias, and bright orange and yellow lilies, the Market's farm tables are filled to overflowing with blossoms in bright neon colors. During the winter months, the Asian farmers bring in boxes and baskets of colorful dried statice. Throughout the day they arrange bouquets and weave flower garlands and wreaths. The items they construct brighten up the long, gray days, serving as a poignant reminder of the summer's bounty.

Make Mine a Double Tall

For years, Seattleites haven't been able to wake up without their beloved morning café latte—a shot or two (or three, for the severely caffeine addicted) of freshly pulled espresso cut with varying amounts of milk. Nowadays the specialty coffee craze has spread well beyond Seattle's borders, down the West Coast and across to the eastern seaboard, into landlocked cities such as Dallas and Atlanta, and even into Canada, Asia, and parts of Europe.

The world's fascination with specialty coffee is due in large part to **Starbucks Coffee Co.**, which opened its very first location in 1971 in the basement of a run-down, wood-frame hotel named Harbor Heights, located just across from the Market's northern boundary. After the old hotel was demolished to make way for a condominium and retail complex, Starbucks was the first tenant to move into the newly renovated Soames-Dunn Building in 1975.

It has been there ever since, and today a commemorative bronze plaque marks "ground zero"—the site of the worldwide coffee chain's inception. The Pike Place space may disappoint Starbucks groupies who make the pilgrimage, for it is a narrow, unassuming storefront with plate glass windows, creaky wood floors, and take-out coffee service only (no seating), nothing like the glitzy flagship stores and Cafe Starbucks of recent years.

Starbucks sold only whole beans at first; espresso drinks were not introduced until 1987. Many coffee cups later, Starbucks is the nation's largest coffee retailer, a shining symbol of how the Market incubates small businesses. In the case of Starbucks, the company has grown into a billion-dollar enterprise responsible for caffeinating seven million Americans each week.

Right: **Seattle's Best Coffee is a popular java haunt in the Market.**

"We Are Farmers!"

FARMERS, WHO PROVIDE THE SPIRITUAL BACKBONE OF THE MARKET, must arrive before eight in the morning, and Judy Duff has been up picking baby lettuces and lemon cucumbers at **Duffield Organic Farm** since four-thirty to meet the strict deadline. Judy, husband Dave, and college-age daughter Deanna have been selling at the Market since 1986. Their farm table is always a delight to the eye as well as to the palate, resplendent with lacy edible flowers in pastel hues, fresh herbs, and jewel-toned bottles of homemade nasturtium and plum vinegar.

Like many Market farmers, the Duffs come in on Fridays and Saturdays, among the busiest days. Participation is spread fairly evenly through the rest of the week, although Wednesdays and Sundays are gaining popularity because of Organic Farmers Day, when certified organic growers set up along Pike Place. As they sell in the open air under tarps and on makeshift wooden tables, the festive atmosphere is reminiscent of the Market's humble beginnings.

Most growers at Pike Place sell between May and November, although many of the farmers selling flowers and processed foods, such as jams and jellies, herb and berry vinegars, cheese, nuts, honey, garlic braids, and holiday wreaths, come in year-round. Farmers' monetary expectations vary widely; a Market-wide survey found that on a "good day" farmers might make anywhere from $100 to $1,000.

At the Duffs' farm table inside the Main Arcade, a hand-lettered sign proclaims "WE ARE FARMERS!" Others describe the origin and taste of each vegetable—exotic items such as haricots verts; baby romaine, Oak Leaf, and French Brunia lettuces; Japanese and Chinese greens; a wide variety of squashes; and different varieties of vine-ripened tomatoes and cucumbers.

Farming is a long tradition in Judy's and Dave's family lines. Judy's antecedents traveled the Oregon Trail in the 1850s and homesteaded thousands of acres near Salem, Oregon. Another branch came to Seattle in 1889 just in time to see the city burn to the ground in the Great Fire. They moved north to Snohomish County to farm. Dave's father still farms in Minnesota.

The agricultural calling is so strong that besides the day-to-day labor involved in raising and selling crops, Judy leads school tours and children's classes on the farm. The Duff family also started the United Farmers Coalition at Pike Place Market (UFC), an advocacy group that provides a voice for the farmers when rules and regulations are updated, maintains a strong farmer presence, and holds educational events.

Left: Parking along Pike Place for farmers or visitors is always tight; the street has been congested since the Market's early days.

At El Mercado Latino during pepper season, you'll find Scotch bonnets and habaneros, the hottest peppers in the world.

OYSTER CHOWDER

The Pacific Northwest is the nation's leading oyster-producing region, with four of six recognizable species—Kumamoto, European flat, Pacific, and Olympia—harvested in the region's waters. In this recipe, fresh oysters and chunks of potatoes swim together happily in a creamy broth—pure Northwest comfort food.

1 jar (10 ounces) fresh shucked oysters

2 tablespoons butter

2 medium leeks, about ¾ pound, white part only, cleaned and sliced ¼ inch thick

1 white or yellow onion, cut into ½-inch dice

2 or 3 baking potatoes, about 1 pound, peeled and cut into ½-inch dice

1½ cups vegetable or chicken stock

½ cup half-and-half

2 cups whole or lowfat milk

1½ teaspoons Worcestershire sauce

Kosher or sea salt and freshly ground white pepper

Ground sweet paprika, for garnish

1. Drain oysters through a fine-meshed sieve placed over a bowl. Save and refrigerate oyster liquid.

2. In a stockpot or Dutch oven, melt 1 tablespoon of the butter over medium heat. Add the oysters and cook 2 to 3 minutes, or until they plump, turning once during cooking time. Remove pan from heat and put oysters and any juice that accumulates in a small bowl. Cover and refrigerate.

3. Return pan to medium heat and melt the remaining 1 tablespoon butter. Add the leeks, onion, and potatoes and cook 5 minutes, or until vegetables are tender-crisp, stirring occasionally. Do not allow vegetables to brown. Add stock, cover, and bring to a boil. Reduce heat and simmer 10 to 15 minutes, or until potatoes are very tender. Remove from heat and allow to cool slightly.

4. Place half of soup in a blender or food processor and pulse until smooth. Return to stockpot along with the reserved oyster liquid, half-and-half, milk, and Worcestershire sauce, and stir until well blended. Add the reserved oysters and liquid and stir gently. Season with salt and pepper. Warm chowder over medium-high heat, stirring occasionally, just until oysters are warmed through.

5. To serve, ladle soup into individual bowls and garnish with paprika.

Serves 4 as an entrée, 8 as an appetizer

Ragin' Cajun in the Market

Chef Danny Delcambre (pronounced "DELL-cum"), a genial, bearded man, was born in New Iberia, Louisiana. The home of Tabasco sauce and the heart of Cajun country, New Iberia is also a population center for people with Usher's Syndrome, a hereditary disease that causes deafness in childhood and blindness in later life, largely among people of Cajun descent. Danny suffers from the disease, which has left him deaf and legally blind.

Despite his affliction, Danny interned with renowned Cajun chef and cookbook author Paul Prudhomme: Danny and wife Holly opened **Delcambre's Ragin' Cajun** in 1993, the first restaurant in the United States owned and operated by a deaf and blind person. The chef and his employees, most of whom are also deaf, communicate using American Sign Language (ASL), as do many of the customers.

Early in the morning, you can catch the chef and his staff stirring the flour and butter to make the dark, smooth roux that forms the base for so much Cajun cooking. Danny works by rote, insisting that all ingredients be lined up in exactly the same place each time so he knows where they are. He cooks by smell and taste, much as other chefs cook by sight.

By 11 A.M., customers begin lining up for chicken and sausage gumbo, jambalaya, black-ened chicken, muffalettas, peach cobbler, and pecan pie, while spirited zydeco music plays in the background and bright chile pepper curtains blow in the breeze created by a couple of lazy ceiling fans. A sparkling black-and-white tile counter flanked by four polished wooden booths, two cozy window tables, and outdoor seating make this restaurant an outpost for authentic New Orleans–inspired cooking as well as a haven for Seattle's deaf community.

In the Beginning—Continued

It was unseasonably rainy on August 17, 1907, the Market's official opening day. The summer dampness soaked the cobbled and planked streets of Seattle and turned unpaved roadways into little more than muddy trails.

H. O. Blanchard, a farmer from near Renton Junction, was the first to brave the unknown commodity known as the Pike Place Market. Fifty shoppers awaited when he arrived at daylight. The crowd swooped down and bought out his produce in minutes, and at better prices than he could ever have gotten from the skinflint wholesalers along Produce Row in the Commission District.

Crescencia Vaca, a farmer from Columbia City, was the second to appear that day. Vaca's produce received a similar welcome. By eight o'clock, several thousand people crowded around

Right: Folksinger Jeanne Towne has performed in the Market since 1976.

the eight or ten wagons that had backed up to the sidewalk. Bankers, mechanics, tradesmen, lawyers, and merchants—people of every class— arrived by carriage, by automobile, and on foot and lined up with their market baskets in hopes of snagging fresh fruits and vegetables.

But it wasn't to be. The throngs of shoppers simply outstripped the farmers' supplies, and the crowds had to be controlled by anxious police. By eleven o'clock, the only produce available came from wagons set up by the dreaded whole-salers from Western Avenue, the very element

MERRY BERRY MEDLEY

Berry season runs long and strong in the Northwest, beginning with small, sweet local strawberries in late spring and ending with local cranberries in the fall. A mix of the sweet gems sprinkled with a crunchy oat topping, baked, and served warm from the oven epitomizes the bounty of summer.

4 cups mixed berries, such as strawberries, blueberries, raspberries, and blackberries

½ to ¾ cup granulated sugar

1 tablespoon lemon juice

1 teaspoon vanilla extract

3 tablespoons quick-cooking tapioca

¾ cup quick-cooking oats

⅓ cup firmly packed brown sugar

2 tablespoons all-purpose flour

½ teaspoon cinnamon

⅛ teaspoon allspice

Pinch salt

¼ cup butter, room temperature and cut into small chunks

Strawberry ice cream or frozen yogurt (optional)

1. Preheat oven to 350°F. Butter a 6-cup baking dish or casserole. In a mixing bowl, gently stir together the berries, ½ cup of the granulated sugar, lemon juice, vanilla, and tapioca. Taste and add remaining ¼ cup sugar if needed. Let stand 15 minutes, then pour fruit into baking dish.

2. Mix together oats, brown sugar, flour, cinnamon, allspice, and salt in a mixing bowl. With a pastry cutter or your hands, work butter into dry ingredients until crumbly. Sprinkle topping evenly over the berries.

3. Bake for 30 to 40 minutes, or until top is golden brown and fruit is bubbly at the edges.

4. To serve, spoon crumble into individual bowls and top with ice cream.

Serves 6

---

the public was trying to bypass. Consumers went home empty-handed rather than patronize the wholesalers' wagons. They would have to wait for another day to shop at the Pike Place Public Market.

The *Seattle Daily Times* published a favorable report about opening day and encouraged farmers to "be on hand bright and early . . . with wagons full of produce at prices that will make glad the hearts of the marketers." The following Saturday, farmers brought wagonloads of produce from Queen Anne Hill, Georgetown, South Park,

Renton, and other nearby farm areas to sell directly to the public.

The crowds were again willing and eager to buy, and the seventy wagons parked on Pike Place sold out their goods within hours. The citizens of Seattle were more than ready to support a venture like the Pike Place Public Market. It was an auspicious beginning.

Roll Call

It's Saturday in the summertime, one of the Market's busiest days, and a throng of artists and craftspeople assembles in the very end of the North Arcade. Some gossip and make jokes. Others, sleepy-eyed, sip coffee and smoke a last cigarette before getting to work. Several stare intently at the large dry-erase board that outlines the 157 daystalls located within the Market.

The Market Master glances up from his clipboard, assesses the crowd, and then looks back down before beginning roll call, the ritualized, rule-bound process of assigning day table space for farmers and crafts vendors. Both groups have areas of day table use defined by City Council contract.

Farmers have priority over craftspeople, and they call the evening before to reserve their favorite stall. By eight the next morning, they are in their assigned spaces, setting up so that the

Left: Handmade costumes, including princess hats, are just a few of the enticements among the craft stalls.

Market Master can collect their daily fees, which run $25 on a Saturday in high season (May through December), $20 on Friday, and less on other weekdays.

Next come the craftspeople, and after poring over attendance lists and records that show who has been selling at the Market the longest, the Master has determined the artists' seniority, expressed in numbers that range from 1 to 160.

When the Market started, a policeman assigned stall space to the farmers on a first-come basis. When that proved too hectic, the office of Market Inspector (changed to Market Master in 1912) was created by the Seattle City Council, and the stalls were allocated by lottery. Then and now, the task of the Market Master is a delicate balancing act; because of all the independent spirits in the Market, the job requires a no-nonsense person who is part mother hen, part policeman, and part referee.

"All right, let's quiet down," the Market Master calls out precisely at 9 A.M. as he begins the crafts roll call.

"Van Dyke," he says.

"Forty," Van Dyke replies, indicating the day table he wants.

Immediately, the Master writes the number 1 in spot number 40 on the dry-erase board.

"Sherwood."

"Seventeen on the wet side."

With its sunny yellow paint job, indoor-outdoor seating along vibrant Post Alley, and simple, fresh, and creative vegetarian-leaning fare, **Sisters European Snacks** has become a favorite of locals, tourists, and Market people, who drop in for their daily cup of soup and moment of gossip. Sisters opened in 1991, brainchild of the Jacobi sisters—Aruna, Mariam, and Nirala—who hail from Frankfurt, Germany.

Their restaurant offers an ever-changing menu that includes European-style *panini* (grilled sandwiches) big enough to share, made-from-scratch soups, and vegetarian salads laden with heart-healthy grains and vegetables. As Aruna explains, "The Market life, with its uniqueness, freshness, colors, and flavors from around the world, is reflected in our food. The every-morning ritual of walking from one end of the Market to the other, with the task of finding out 'What are we going to cook today?' is still exciting after all these years."

The number 2 goes on the dry-erase board in spot 17.

"Hansen."

"Fifty-nine."

The process continues until all the spaces are assigned. Seniority numbers 1 to 20 choose the most desirable spaces in the North Arcade. The numbers 21 to 40 usually sell on the Desimone Bridge, whose dry, covered tables are reserved exclusively for craftspeople—no farmers. Higher numbers take their chances with what is left, often winding up on the dreaded "slabs." These uncovered concrete ledges that jut out over the sidewalk north along Pike Place are considered the least desirable spaces because they're open to the elements and have the smallest amount of foot traffic.

Artists started coming to the Market en masse in the late 1960s and early 1970s, as the number of farmers diminished. The Pike Place Market crafts community has evolved into the largest permanent crafts display in the Northwest, a unique grouping of craftspeople, artists, and artisans that meets every day in the same location. Dozens of trades are practiced, from costume making to stained glass, goldsmithing to gemcutting, quilting to pottery, photography to woodblock prints. In many cases, the artists have come up with witty or whimsical business names such as Gone to Pot (pottery), Primal Screens (clothing), the Kaleidoscope Guy at the Market (kaleidoscopes), and Ear Reverence (jewelry). Some claim it is the largest artisan community in the United States.

Right: Drop your quarters in the coin box and the velvet curtain parts to reveal the secrets of the Giant Shoe Museum.

The DownUnder

The DownUnder is a rabbit's warren of more than fifty antique stores, gift shops, and restaurants. Through the years, this hub of commercial activity has housed a post office, a sugar stall (a loss leader underwritten by Market management), a branch of the public library, a doughnut shop, a lard rendering plant, a print shop, repair shops, numerous secondhand stores, and "Madame Nora's Temple of Destiny." The Market renovation in the 1970s brought polished fir and maple floors, better lighting, and reinforcement of the heavy wooden timbers that support the structure.

Today, the DownUnder is a universe of unique shops for the young and young at heart—Craft

Emporium, Sweeties Candies, Hands of the World, Outback Opal, Market Coins. But perhaps most child oriented are Pike Place Magic Shop, Golden Age Collectables, Charlotte's Web, Women's Hall of Fame, and Old Seattle Paperworks' Giant Shoe Museum.

Old Seattle Paperworks has been in business for more than twenty years, but it looks as though it might have been around since the Market's inception. Its space is packed with rare prints, early photography, antique postcards, turn-of-the-century magazines, advertising art, old-timey cutouts, postcards, and stationery stacked in vintage wooden cubbyholes and shelves. Some of it is original, some reproduction. A few years back, owner John Hanawalt incorporated the **World Famous Giant Shoe Museum** into his storefront. It is like a circus sideshow, with viewing windows and heavy curtains. "The Greatest Shoe on Earth" claims to house the world's largest collection of giant shoes and related history. One pair was worn by the world's tallest man, Robert Wadlow, who at 8 feet, 11.1 inches had big shoes to fill.

Rod Dyke has probably heard the lament "If only my mother hadn't thrown away my comic books" more than anyone in the Northwest. His response? "If all the mothers had saved their children's comic books, I wouldn't have a job today."

For twenty-eight years, Rod has owned **Golden Age Collectables**, the Northwest's oldest and largest comic book store, with a reputed one million copies in stock. Life-size cutouts of Betty Boop, Marilyn Monroe, the Three Stooges, and the cast from *Star Wars* greet you outside the present-day shop. Besides current comic books, back issues, and underground comics, the store sells other collectibles such as toys, autographs, sports memorabilia, buttons, posters, robots, and movie scripts and memorabilia.

By special appointment only, Rod will show you the shop's most expensive items—a Superman #1 comic book in "very fine" condition that is priced at $85,000 and a Batman #1 comic book in "fine" condition that could be yours for $35,000. They're stored in a bank vault for security, and in archival Mylar to preserve the ink and paper for posterity.

Pike Place Magic Shop is a resource center for aspiring, amateur, and professional magicians. In this fun, jam-packed place of enthusiasm and wonder, turn-of-the-century magic posters and photos of famous magicians grace the walls. Demonstrations of prestidigitation (sleight of hand) are a regular occurrence, and "the secret is part of the sale."

Open since the early 1970s, the longest-running magic shop in the Pacific Northwest is co-owned by resident magicians Sheila "Magic Lady" Lyon and Darryl "The Amazing" Beckmann. They are

Left: More than fifty shops, including antique stores, gift shops, and restaurants, make up the Market's intriguing DownUnder section.

GRASSLANDS LAMB STEW

Chunks of grass-fed lamb and lentils meld into a hearty, distinctive stew when simmered with vegetables, dried cherries, and a fruity Washington State merlot. Using lamb sirloin, although a more costly cut of meat than lamb neck or shoulder, ensures meltingly tender results.

8 whole cloves

½ teaspoon black peppercorns

1 to 2 tablespoons olive or vegetable oil

1 pound lamb sirloin, cut into bite-size pieces

1 white or yellow onion, cut in half and quartered

2 carrots, cut on the diagonal into ¼-inch slices

3 cloves garlic, peeled and halved

½ cup brown or green lentils, rinsed and picked over for debris

2 tomatoes, about ¾ pounds, cored and chopped, or 1 can (14½ ounces) whole tomatoes, chopped

1½ cups good-quality, fruity red wine, such as Washington State merlot, or 1½ cups beef broth

1 heaping tablespoon dried cherries or cranberries

1 bay leaf

½ teaspoon fresh thyme or ¼ teaspoon dried thyme, crumbled

Pinch ground cinnamon

Kosher or sea salt and freshly ground black pepper

4 servings cooked white or brown rice or egg noodles

1. Make a bouquet garni by cutting a 4 by 4-inch piece of cheesecloth and placing the cloves and peppercorns in the middle. Gather up the sides, tie with kitchen twine, and set aside.

2. Heat 1 tablespoon of the oil in a large stockpot or Dutch oven over medium-high heat, and add lamb. Cook 8 to 10 minutes, or until lamb is browned on all sides. Remove lamb from pan and reserve. Pour off all but 1 tablespoon of fat or, if little remains, add another tablespoon of oil.

3. Add onions, carrots, garlic, and bouquet garni to pan and cook 5 to 7 minutes or until tender-crisp, stirring occasionally. Adjust heat if the vegetables start to stick. Add lamb, lentils, tomatoes, wine, dried cherries, bay leaf, thyme, and cinnamon. Stir, bring to a low simmer, and cover stockpot. Cook for 1¼ hours, or until meat and lentils are tender. Do not allow mixture to boil, or meat will toughen. Season to taste with salt and pepper.

4. To serve, remove bouquet garni and bay leaf and spoon stew over cooked rice or noodles.

Serves 4 to 6

on hand to advise, demonstrate, and explain the many magic kits and paraphernalia in stock: props for the beginner to the pro, cards and coins, books and teaching videos, juggling equipment, dummies and ventriloquism supplies, clowning supplies, jokes and gags, and much more. Even the names are evocative—"Eye of the Idol," "The Pocket Levitator," and "Aces in Their Faces."

The **Women's Hall of Fame** is a 160-square-foot space filled with books, bumper stickers, posters, games, and T-shirts, all with a historical, feminist, or multicultural theme. African-American histories and children's books, puzzles, and historically accurate paper doll sets make this a favorite resource for parents and teachers.

Charlotte's Web, which has been in business since 1969, offers the largest collection of limited-edition African-American figurines in the country. Besides the extensive array of black heritage figures and dolls, other treasures found in the store include miniatures, tea sets, angels, and animals.

Right: The mechanical fortune-teller "Knows All/Tells All" at her post in front of Pike Place Magic Shop.

The Queen of the Market

Since its inception in 1907, the Pike Place Market has been a mecca for successive waves of immigrants to the Pacific Northwest and an incubator for cuisines from across the world.

About half of the farmers in the early years were native-born Americans; most of the rest were newly arrived from Europe, although there were some Chinese and a growing number of Japanese and Filipinos.

Italian immigrants played a major part in the Market's development. According to the late Angelo Pellegrini, a University of Washington

English professor and noted food writer, the Italian farmers were "born practitioners of selective breeding, using always the finest [seed] stock for reproduction, without having read Darwin on the subject." They raised crops and carted them to the Market: "a variety of herbaceous edibles and culinary herbs that were unknown to native Americans: turnip and mustard greens, kale, two kinds of endive, arugula, celery root, savoy cabbage, dandelion, salsify, garlic; and such aromatics as sage, rosemary, thyme, oregano, parsley, basil, hot and mild cherry pepper."

Part of the immigrant farmer's job was to teach customers how to prepare unfamiliar foods so they would buy them, and the Italian farmers excelled at marketing their goods. Angelo described Angela Maria Ferrucci, active in the Market from 1920 to 1960, who "explained to patrons what her unfamiliar vegetables were and how to prepare them for the table; how to aromatize sliced tomatoes with a sprinkling of minced oregano; how to make a salad dressing of olive oil, wine vinegar, and garlic juice; how to enhance the flavor of roasts of pork, chicken, and ham with rosemary, sage, and garlic."

Pasqualina Verdi, who sold in the Market for almost thirty-five years, was Ferrucci's natural successor. Finding herself a widow with an eight-year-old son, Pasqualina emigrated from Avellino, Italy, to Seattle in 1949 to marry Dominic Verdi, a farmer and widower with eight children of his own. They raised zucchini, scallions, and other vegetables on their farm in south Seattle, but when it became apparent that the family could not make a living selling their produce to wholesalers, Pasqualina began coming to the Market in 1955.

Pasqualina was the prototypical Italian farm mother, complete with ruddy cheeks, a kerchief around her hair, and a stocky build. She didn't speak a word of English, and at first she could only count and make change. But over the years, in her engaging, if bewildering, mix of Italian and English, she managed to teach several generations of Seattleites the secrets of Italian cooking, often by sneaking unfamiliar vegetables (free of charge) into unsuspecting customers' bags in hopes that they would try them at home.

In her later years Pasqualina was dubbed the "Queen of the Market," and her son Mike is still an active Market farmer.

A Pig's Life

Rachel, the Market's life-size bronze piggy bank, is a world-renowned icon located just under the Market clock. Besides serving as a civic landmark and convenient meeting spot for locals and visitors from around the world, the pig with a purpose accepts pocket change in her coin slot. Children of all ages contribute about $8,000 each year in pennies, quarters, and checks, as well as pesos, lira, yen, and rials, to benefit the Market Foundation. The foundation helps the ten thousand low-income and elderly people in the Market neighborhood with expenses for food, medicine, housing, and child care. Rachel, the sow with a social sensibility, has been bringing home the bacon since she was installed on August 17, 1986, the Market's seventy-ninth anniversary.

Washingtonians, who harbor a certain suspicion of Californians, may be dismayed to learn that the flesh-and-blood Rachel the pig who

Right: Children of all ages are drawn to Rachel, the Market's life-size bronze piggy bank.

inspired the statue was born near San Francisco. Luckily, she traveled to Washington in the back of a convertible just a few months after her birth and quickly adapted to life on the Whidbey Island farm of owners Joyce and Bob McArthur, producing native Washington piglets at a prodigious pace.

Market Foundation board member Shirley Collins, former owner of Sur La Table, came up with the idea for the Market's giant piggy bank. When Whidbey Island resident Georgia Gerber was commissioned to sculpt the "perfect porker," she searched Western Washington high and low until she found Rachel, who, when the statue was finished, outweighed it by two hundred pounds. Even though her form was immortalized in bronze, the live Rachel was a real ham and enjoyed basking in the limelight at county fairs, greeting visitors at the farm, and hosting Market events. Her crowning moment came when she won the 1985 Island County Fair.

In the summer of 1991, at the age of eleven, Rachel's porcine heart and arthritic bones gave out. Luckily, daughter Rebecca was waiting in the wings to take over her mantle. The Reading Terminal Market in downtown Philadelphia has borrowed the Rachel fund-raising idea with a bronze pig of its own. Both Philbert and Rachel enjoy celebrating March 1, National Pig Day.

Left: Bouquets in plastic buckets line the North Arcade beginning at seven each morning.

Low-Flying Fish

Under the Market clock and behind Rachel the Pig, there's always a festive air at **Pike Place Fish,** which was founded in 1930 and in recent years has become known worldwide as "the home of the low-flying fish." While longtime street musician Jonny Hahn bangs away at his piano in one of the prime musician's spots, the Pike Place fishmongers' chorus of voices urges passersby to "stop, stop, stop" and "buy, buy, buy."

"One sockeye, packed to go," they chant in singsong unison when an order is placed. The clerk out front hoists a glinting salmon from the icy pile and tosses it skyward. Somehow, his cohorts behind the counter (almost) always manage to catch the cold, slippery charge—with a whap—like a baseball in a catcher's mitt. "One sockeye, packed to go," the fishmongers chant as the order is wrapped.

Many of the tourists can't resist the floor show and end up buying a slice of Northwest nirvana, in the form of a salmon or some Dungeness crabs, to take back to Nebraska or Tokyo and share with family and friends. Packaged in leakproof, odorproof containers, their purchases can be carried on a plane, checked as luggage, or shipped by overnight air express. Lined with blue gel "ice" packs, the containers are guaranteed to keep the contents fresh for up to forty-eight hours.

Left: Beware the low-flying fish under the Market clock at Pike Place Fish.

Right: Wild coho salmon run from July through October, peaking in September.

Even locals who have long since grown blasé about the noisy seafood-throwing spectacle often pause for a stolen moment in front of the open-air displays to gaze at the geoduck with its elephant-trunk neck, the barnacle-encrusted oysters piled six inches high, or the unsightly monkfish that gapes over ice, its jaws propped open so that row upon jagged row of triangular teeth are exposed.

Tourists are not so fortunate, for when they stoop down to examine the monstrous monkfish, the fishmongers pull the hidden string tied to the creature's tail. Screams ring out as the giant fish leaps from its bed of ice. The unsuspecting have been known to run from the Market, never to return again.

Moo in the Market

The Fairmount Apartments at First and Stewart were once home to the Fairmount Creamery, and the modern-day **Pike Place Market Creamery** carries on the tradition in grand style with a wide array of milk and milk-related products. Throughout the day, the young, fit employees make deliveries to fellow Market vendors,

ASIAN VEGETABLE CURRY

This recipe highlights the vegetables and herbs that the Asian farmers offer in abundance on the day tables. The vegetables cook quickly, so be sure everything is chopped and measured before you start.

4 heads baby bok choy

1 can (14 ounces) unsweetened regular or light coconut milk

3 tablespoons green curry paste

1 medium carrot, cut on the diagonal into ¼-inch slices

1 medium Japanese eggplant, halved lengthwise and cut on the diagonal into ¼-inch slices

½ red bell pepper, halved vertically and sliced ¼ inch thick

¼ pound snow peas, tails removed and cut in half on the diagonal

8 large Thai, green (Italian), or purple basil leaves, coarsely chopped

8 kaffir lime leaves or ½ teaspoon freshly grated lime zest

1 tablespoon Thai fish sauce (nam pla)

1 tablespoon palm sugar or dark brown sugar

6 ounces firm regular or lowfat tofu, cut into bite-size pieces

4 cups cooked jasmine rice

2 tablespoons chopped cilantro

1. To prepare the bok choy, trim the stem end and pull the stalks away from the core, discarding any broken or blemished leaves. Cut the leaves from the stems, leaving as little green as possible on the stems. Rinse both parts separately and drain well. A little water can remain on the bok choy without compromising the dish.

2. In a wok or large saucepan, bring the coconut milk and curry paste to a gentle boil over medium-high heat. Add the carrot, eggplant, red pepper, and snow peas and cook 4 minutes, stirring occasionally.

3. Reduce heat to medium, add the bok choy stems, and cook 2 minutes, stirring occasionally. Add the bok choy leaves and cook 2 minutes more, stirring occasionally.

4. Add the basil, lime leaves, fish sauce, and palm sugar and stir well. Taste the sauce and add more fish sauce or palm sugar if desired. Add the tofu and cook 2 minutes more, or until the bok choy leaves just begin to wilt and the tofu is warmed through. Do not overstir or the tofu will break up.

5. To serve, divide the rice among individual large soup or pasta bowls and ladle the stew over the rice. Sprinkle with cilantro and serve immediately.

Serves 4

restaurants, and espresso stands throughout the downtown area. Cowbells clank as handtrucks stacked high with crates of milk, cream, and dairy products are wheeled up the cobbled inclines and down the wooden floors of the Market.

In operation since 1977, the Creamery is a place where regular customers can count on a smile, a kind word, and a hug from proprietor and self-described "head milkmaid" Nancy Nipples. Children of all ages love to stop in front of the egg case, which features not only brown and white eggs from free-range chickens, but pastel-hued aracauna eggs, giant ostrich and emu eggs, tiny spotted quail eggs, and duck, goose, and turkey eggs.

The milk case highlights cow's milk in glass bottles, raw goat's milk, thick Devonshire cream imported from England, crème fraîche, and mascarpone, an Italian-style cream cheese. Don't miss the "Dairy Moo-morabilia" museum, a kitschy collection of cows, chickens, and related cartoons donated by Nancy's loyal customers and fans.

Just steps away from the Creamery is another mecca for dairy lovers—**Quality Cheese**. Stop by for a fresh-cut wedge or two from their collection of more than 130 cheeses from the Northwest, United States, and around the world.

Right: The Market community is composed of all sorts of unique personalities.

HOLIDAY SPECIAL
SWEET
RAINIER
CHERRIES
$299
POUND

SOLID
BEEFSTEAK
TOMATOES
99¢
POUND

FRESH
WHITE
BI COLOR
CORN

FRESH
TENDER
BEANS

UMS
ERRY
MATOES

GOOD AFTERNOON

Time to Pray

THE UPPER FLOOR OF THE ECONOMY MARKET IS HOME TO THE MARKET MINISTRY, more properly called the **Chapel of St. Martha and St. Mary of Bethany.** The chapel is open to the public for prayer and meditation Monday through Friday and Sunday. It serves Market residents, business people, and anyone who wants to come in off the street. The chapel regulars include a number of homeless Hispanic men. Many dream of working the fishing boats in Alaska and have holed up in Seattle in hopes of being hired on and sent north by their employers.

The ministry is run by the Episcopal Diocese of Olympia under the capable leadership of the Reverend Susan O'Shea. Madre Susan, as she is called by many of "her people," is an engaging and dedicated woman who knows about life on the streets from firsthand experience. The victim of an abusive home, she was out on her own by the age of seven. The young girl hung out at the Market and credits other homeless people, whom she dubbed her "grandparents," with raising her. She remembers that the merchants "kept me and my dog in boiled shrimp."

Today, Madre Susan is out of the office, but her spirit of caring and goodwill permeates the chapel. Light from the plate glass windows that overlook First Avenue bounces about the ivory walls. Spanish soap operas and game shows, which the reverend videotapes for her followers because they remind them of home, play on the television. Two parakeets chirp excitedly in their cage. A small fountain burbles in front of a simple altar.

A half dozen men from Bolivia, El Salvador, and Ecuador sit on cloth-draped couches, relaxing and talking. Others play chess or checkers at tables covered with flowered oilcloth. Beth McCann, an interior designer who volunteers at the chapel once a week, stands up, a signal that today's noontime service is about to begin. She's a pretty, petite woman with frosted hair and large gold hoop earrings. Her long-sleeved denim shirt, vest, and G. H. Bass slacks are casual yet chic. This is her fourth year at the chapel.

"*Es la hora de rezar,*" Beth says in halting Spanish, as she explains that *rezar* means "to pray."

She leads the first Bible selection in Spanish, then instructs Ignacio, one of the chapel's regulars, to read the next verse.

He's a squat man with long black hair and a khaki-colored raincoat that falls to his knees. He seems at once shy yet proud to read Ecclesiastes in front of his peers. All the men join in chorus to exult in Spanish, "The Lord takes pleasure in his people; he adorns the humble with victory. Alleluia!"

When the readings are over about fifteen minutes later, Beth blesses the men and invokes them to go forth into the world rejoicing in the glory of God. There's a brief silence, then the men get up for a cup of coffee with canned evaporated milk (another reminder of their homeland), head for the phone, or resume their board games.

"The shelters kick homeless people out at six in the morning, and they can't go back until nightfall," Beth explains as she sits down at her desk. "Then the public complains about people on the streets. The chapel offers the homeless a safe haven—a spot that is peaceful. It really helps them change their lives. We try to do everything possible to help people get back on their feet, and we encourage the community to help each other. It's not what you get at regular churches."

In 1979, when the City of Seattle threatened to force the Pike Place Market fishmongers to put their wares behind glass to meet health code requirements, a special ordinance was passed to keep the fish on ice and out in front!

GLAZED ASPARAGUS

So much asparagus is grown in the Yakima Valley in Eastern Washington that it's fondly referred to as "Yakima grass." It's rumored that if you pass through asparagus country during growing season, you can hear the spears growing in the fields.

1 tablespoon canola or vegetable oil
1 tablespoon regular or low-sodium soy sauce
1 tablespoon brown sugar or maple syrup
1 tablespoon Dijon mustard

1½ teaspoons prepared horseradish
1 pound fresh asparagus, hard ends removed, remaining portion rinsed, drained, and patted dry

1. Preheat the broiler. Lightly oil a baking sheet and set aside.

2. In a small bowl, mix together oil, soy sauce, brown sugar, and mustard. Add horseradish and blend thoroughly.

3. Arrange asparagus spears in a single layer on baking sheet without crowding. Hold asparagus down by the stem ends and brush top 3 to 4 inches lightly with glaze. Broil 3 to 4 inches from heat source for 3 minutes, remove from oven, turn asparagus, brush with glaze again, and broil for 3 minutes more. Repeat this process until spears are lightly browned and tender at the stem end when a metal skewer or the tip of a small, sharp knife is inserted. Thin asparagus will take from 6 to 9 minutes, thick spears up to 15 minutes.

4. Arrange spears on a communal platter or divide among individual plates and serve straight from the oven or at room temperature as an appetizer or side dish.

Serves 4 to 6

The World Within a Market Block

A visit to the block of the Market between Virginia and Stewart is like an around-the-world culinary tour, where the only dilemma is deciding which cuisine to enjoy first.

Saigon Restaurant is one of the oldest Vietnamese restaurants in town, a favorite of area chefs and Market workers. The atmosphere is no-frills, with seating at the counter or small tables in back, but owner Vinh Pham and her expertly prepared Vietnamese soups, salads, seafood, and vegetarian dishes more than make up for the stark ambiance. The food here is low in fat and healthy, loaded with bean sprouts,

fresh cilantro, and chopped tomatoes; portions are generous, inexpensive, and served quickly.

A *souk* is a marketplace in northern Africa or the Middle East. The Market's own **Souk** is a mecca for those wishing to purchase Middle Eastern, Indian, or Pakistani spices and delicacies for use at home. The sagging shelves groan under the weight of dozens of brands of chutneys and pickles; quince, date, eggplant, and fig jams; dried apricot paste from Syria; mustard oil; and *pappadams* (fried bread). Wooden barrels hold numerous colors and varieties of basmati rice, legumes, and lentils. A final reminder of home for Seattle's Indian and Arabic émigrés are the newspapers and magazines, audio and video tapes, and calendars written in Arabic as well as in several Indian tongues.

Located on sloping Stewart Street, just a stone's throw from bustling Pike Place, **Japanese Gourmet** is a simple but welcoming oasis, featuring sushi and sashimi (don't miss the Pike Place Market roll); traditional dishes such as tempura, teriyaki, and sukiyaki; vegetarian options; and noodle dishes and *donburi* (boiled rice with assorted toppings).

Shopping at the **Mexican Grocery** is a south-of-the-border treat: vanilla extract imported from Mexico, *queso fresco* (fresh cheese), and *masa* (a special dough ground from lime-treated corn kernels, used to make tortillas, tacos, enchiladas,

Left: The Souk is a source of Indian, Pakistani, and Middle Eastern spices and specialty foods.

and tamales) are just a few of the items to be found. Fresh red and green salsas are made on the premises several times a day. By pairing them with tortilla chips, fresh tortillas, tamales, and the colorful piñatas that dangle overhead, you could put together a party for six or sixty at a moment's notice, creating lots of fun in the process.

The scent of garlic lures you into **Cucina Fresca,** where chef/co-owner Jay Beattie and his staff bustle about the commercial kitchen stirring pots of marinara and alfredo sauce, rolling out sheets of fresh pasta, baking yeasty pans of focaccia and garlic bread, and stuffing homemade ravioli with creative fillings.

The hefty glass-and-mahogany display case will soon overflow with an ever-changing selection of Mediterranean-inspired take-out items. Options for the perfect picnic or take-out meal might include orzo chicken salad, tandoori chicken, calamari salad, panini, or tortellini pesto. Biscotti, tiramisu, and lemon cheesecake make sweet finales. There is a small seating area with a counter and stools facing the bustling kitchen, but most people take their purchases home to eat, or carry them across the street to Victor Steinbrueck Park for a picnic lunch.

Ahmet and Semra Yavuz, who hail from Turkey, enjoy introducing their customers to specialties from their homeland and the

CURRIED APPLES WITH CIDER CREAM

Combining several varieties of heirloom apples yields the most flavor in this apple compote. The touch of curry powder warms the spirit on cool autumn days.

3 large, crisp heirloom apples, about 1½ pounds, preferably a mix of several hardy varieties such as Braeburn, Granny Smith, Gravenstein, Fuji, Pippin, or Criterion	*1 teaspoon mild curry powder*
	½ teaspoon ground cinnamon
	¼ teaspoon ground allspice
	¼ cup sugar
1 tablespoon butter	*2 tablespoons golden raisins (optional)*

1. To prepare the apples, rinse and pat dry but do not peel. Core the apples, cut into quarters, and cut the quarters into bite-sized pieces.

2. Melt the butter in a large skillet or Dutch oven over medium-high heat. Add the curry powder, cinnamon, and allspice and cook for 1 to 2 minutes, stirring constantly with a wooden spoon, until the spices are aromatic. Add the sugar and optional raisins and mix well, then add the apples and stir until they are covered with the sugar/spice syrup. Cover and cook 7 to 10 minutes, or until apples are tender but not mushy, stirring occasionally.

3. To serve, place apples in individual dessert dishes and top with Cider Cream.

Serves 4 to 6

CIDER CREAM

1 cup good-quality apple cider or ¼ cup apple juice concentrate, thawed	*1 cup whipping cream*

1. Bring the apple cider to a boil in a small saucepan. (If using apple juice concentrate instead of cider, skip this step and begin with step 2.) Cook 7 to 10 minutes, or until mixture is reduced to about ¼ cup. Remove from heat and allow to cool.

2. Beat whipping cream until stiff, then fold in cider (or apple juice concentrate) until thoroughly mixed. Keep refrigerated until ready to use, up to three days.

Makes 1½ cups sauce

The Market is open from 9 A.M. to 6 P.M. Monday through Saturday and from 11 A.M. to 5 P.M. Sunday. Many businesses keep longer hours. Sunday is a voluntary day for merchants, and some businesses remain closed.

Mediterranean at **Turkish Delight.** Try the thick lentil soup, *borek* (savory pastries stuffed with spinach and feta), or a chicken gyro—minced chicken molded around a spit, vertically roasted, sliced, and rolled in pita bread with cucumber-yogurt sauce.

Save room for dessert, which might be a couple of pieces of *rahat loukoum,* or Turkish delight. One of the oldest confections in the world, this mixture of fruit juices, gelatin, and nuts comes in several flavors and is made on-site. An airy slice of baklava is another sweet option. Savor a super-strong slug of Turkish coffee, heavily sweetened and as thick as mud by the time you get to the bottom of the small demitasse cup, for a jolting finale to this around-the-world tour in a single Market block.

Foodie's Delight

From a run-down thrift shop on canted Pine Street sprang **Sur La Table,** one of America's premier kitchenware stores. National cookbook authors and celebrity chefs make a pilgrimage to the cluttered kitchen shop with a Continental flair when they're passing through Seattle on promotional tours. Even the grande dame of French cooking herself, Julia Child, stops by to sign books and chat with the crowd whenever she's in town.

They come from far and wide because Sur La Table is a foodie's delight, where you can find items that literally aren't carried anywhere else. Snake your way through the labyrinth of French copper cookware, German and Japanese cutlery, table linens imported from China and India, dinnerware, glassware, cookbooks, and the extensive baking department, and just try to hold on to your wallet.

Esoteric items such as an *herbes de Provence* mill ("used on tables throughout the south of France"), a Parmesan knife ("whose oversized blade is shaped perfectly to confidently cut a wedge of delicious Parmesan"), or ravioli stamps ("efficient tools to seal, press, and mark ravioli so that it can be cut evenly") tempt even the most determined shopper.

Hats Off to Sharon

Sharon Hagerty is an intense young woman with pale skin, eyes the color of pennies, and dark hair covered by a chic fedora. Like many young women of her generation, Sharon delighted in getting a new Easter bonnet every spring. She began collecting hats as a youth, but it wasn't until she attended community college in San Francisco that she realized she could turn her interest in hats into a career.

Sharon landed in the heart of New York City's

Garment District, where she earned a millinery certificate from the prestigious Fashion Institute of Technology. After that, she found herself back in San Francisco, where she taught millinery at the Academy of Art, made hats, and waitressed to make ends meet. Her reputation spread as her work appeared in fashion magazines, movies, theater productions, and fashion shows.

But the drive to excel in her profession propelled Sharon to Seattle, where she met Herman Helmun, the owner of **Eclipse Hat Shop.** Herman was "an icon in the dying craft of hat restoration." Although he had contracted polio at age eleven, he learned hat renovation as part of Roosevelt's Depression-era New Deal program and took over Eclipse in 1949.

It was an unlikely duo, the savvy young woman from San Francisco and the elderly man who lived and worked in the Market. Often he ran over her feet with his motorized

Left: Sharon Hagerty is the owner of Eclipse Hat Shop, which has operated since 1949.

wheelchair, but they enjoyed exchanging trade secrets and tips.

"I'd been a long-distance apprentice of Herman's through the mail, over the telephone, and on my visits to Seattle. I'd come to Seattle, stay at Pensione Nichols in the Market, and sit in Herman's shop all weekend, watching him, talking to him, feeding him, hanging out with him. We'd talk about tools, such as this conformer, which measures the exact circumference of the head," she explained as she adjusted a hat-shaped apparatus whose metal fingers splayed open to encase her head like a weird medieval torture device.

"Or this egg iron, which is like an egg-shaped curling iron that heats up and conforms to the inside of a hat. Or these blacksmithing shears, whose bent ends allow you to cut on a curve. Then I'd go back to my bed-and-breakfast and take notes and get excited about purchasing some hat blocks or ribbon and going back to my life in San Francisco."

In 1997, Sharon's life changed abruptly when the ailing Herman decided to sell his shop. Months later, she gave up her apartment and teaching post in San Francisco and said goodbye to waitressing. She was the new owner of the venerable Eclipse Hat Shop.

The old shop was almost sagging under the weight of five hundred wooden hat blocks for

Down a little-used hallway that leads from the First Level DownUnder into the Main Market hangs a billboard-sized poster of Claude Alexander Conlin Sr., **"The Great Alexander."** Alexander's pale head is wrapped in a striped turban. From his perch on high, his riveting green eyes stare into a crystal ball held by a skeletal hand. Scenes of birth, marriage, and death are depicted in the crystal ball, for Alexander is the man who "KNOWS ALL, TELLS ALL."

"The Man Who Knows" started his career in Seattle at the turn of the twentieth century and quickly became a vaudeville headliner who crisscrossed the nation. He performed illusions during the first half of his show. The second half was devoted to answering the questions and solving the problems of his curious followers.

Alexander did well as a magician/mentalist. His salary of $6,000 a week in 1916 had tripled to $18,000 by 1919, and during his lifetime the superstar is rumored to have made $4 million. But all that money couldn't buy him love. The mentalist should have seen it coming, for he married nine times and died in 1954.

ARUGULA-BASIL PESTO

Pesto, a combination of fresh herbs, hard cheese, nuts, and olive oil that originated in Genoa, is a kitchen staple nowadays, but it must have seemed strangely exotic when the Market's Italian farmers introduced it to Seattle. This version includes arugula, a pungent, peppery Italian green also known as rocket.

2 cloves garlic, halved

1 cup tightly packed fresh basil leaves, about 1 ounce, rinsed and patted dry

1 to 2 cups tightly packed fresh arugula leaves, about 2 ounces, rinsed and patted dry (see note)

½ cup extra-virgin olive oil

3 tablespoons pine nuts, walnuts, or almonds

Pinch kosher or sea salt

½ cup freshly grated imported Parmesan cheese, preferably Parmigiano-Reggiano

2 tablespoons freshly grated Pecorino Romano cheese

1. In a food processor, pulse garlic until finely chopped. Add basil, arugula, olive oil, nuts, and salt, and pulse until fairly smooth, scraping down sides of processor as needed.

2. Remove pesto from food processor and stir in cheeses. Taste and adjust seasonings. Use immediately or transfer to a jar with a tight-fitting lid and refrigerate for up to 1 week.

Makes 1⅓ cups

Note: The flavor of arugula can vary considerably depending on the species and time of year it is harvested. If the arugula you have is very peppery, use 1 cup; if mild, use 2 cups.

Left: The Public Market sign casts its shadow on the historic Triangle Building, which in earlier times served as the Market Hotel.

everything from homburgs to fedoras, countless skeins of antique ribbon, and all the unusual tools collected by Herman over his forty-eight years in business. There had been no capital renovations in twenty years, and the whole place desperately needed a good dusting, a coat of paint, and some tender loving care.

Sharon worked on renovations until the store's opening day. Although hospitalized, Herman convinced his doctors he was well enough to travel and made a surprise appearance via gurney. After turning over the reins to Sharon, Herman moved to a nursing home in Bremerton, Washington, and began attending college. His spirits seemed bright, but at age eighty-one, his body simply gave out.

A sandwich, a cup of soup, and a slab of pie at **Three Girls Bakery** is a time-honored Seattle tradition, served up by waiters and waitresses with an attitude. The chicken salad is made with poultry that's roasted each morning and then mixed with celery and pineapple; meatloaf aficionados consider the cold meatloaf sandwich the city's best rendition, as rich as pâté; and the chili is a menu staple. Corned beef, pastrami, roast beef, egg salad, turkey, ham, salami, tuna, and liverwurst with a choice of trimmings are served on sourdough, nine-grain, dark or light rye bread or buns. Present owner Jack Levy also sells bread by the loaf, cookies, macaroons, and other bakery items assembled from the "who's who" list of Seattle bakeries. A Market original, Three Girls started in the Corner Market building in 1912.

"He wanted to stay alive to see the store a success, and that's really touching," Sharon muses. "But he was the success. He kept this business going, had an excellent reputation, and did the best work. He was nice to everybody and loved the Market people."

Little Italy

Like an Italian shopkeeper straight out of central casting, Louie DeLaurenti hustles behind the counter at **DeLaurenti Specialty Food Markets,** cutting deli meat to order, helping a customer choose among twenty-one types of bulk olives, or weighing a pound of imported cheese. His short green jacket is emblazoned with his family name, his eyes sparkle behind wire-rimmed glasses, his mustache is just so.

An afternoon shopping spree at DeLaurenti is like a visit to the Italian grocery stores in South Philadelphia or Little Italy in New York City. The pungent, spicy scent of cured meats mixes with the yeasty odor of fresh-baked breads trucked in from the city's best bakeries. Olive oils in every hue of yellow and green, along with ruby-toned bottles of balsamic vinegar, line an entire wall. Amaretti in colorful cans, packages of ladyfingers, and biscotti in huge glass jars tempt the sweet tooth. If price is not an object, ask for the costly bottles of balsamic vinegar hidden safely behind the counter or for the white winter truffles imported from Italy. Surprisingly, the cramped, two-level space with impossibly narrow aisles also houses a wine shop, a casual Italian cafe, and a take-out pizza window.

The DeLaurenti family has been in the Market since 1928, when Angelina "Mama" Mustello opened a small store on the Mezzanine

Right: The LaSalle Apartments, which once housed an upscale bordello, today provides low-income housing for the Market's elderly population.

Level of the Market where Ivacco Foods, a bulk food store, is now located. Angelina, an immigrant from Abruzzi, Italy, sold pasta, eggs, butter, and Italian cheeses to members of Seattle's ethnic populations, including the Italian, Greek, Jewish, French, and Slavic communities.

Angelina's daughter, Mamie-Marie, met the dashing Peter DeLaurenti, a deliveryman for Seattle French Bakery, while working for her mother. Their son, Louie, started working at the store, then known as Pete's Italian Grocery, in the 1940s, when he was eleven years old. As the store prospered over the years, the site simply became too small to hold all of the specialty products and fresh foods it stocked.

In 1973 Louie bought the business, changed the name to DeLaurenti Specialty Food Markets, and relocated to the old Bartell drugstore space at the Market's main entrance. Today DeLaurenti anchors the corner at First and Pike and has a second location in downtown Bellevue, Washington. Life seems to have come full circle for Louie, whose first memory of the Market is shining shoes out in front of Bartell Drugs when he was ten years old.

Particularly Pike Place

Many of the small businesses in the Market are unique operations that exist solely because of the owner's singular philosophy, imagination, or strong business contacts.

Stepping over the threshold at **Enchanted Garden** is like visiting a foreign world. King

Left: MarketSpice, which opened in 1911, today sells hundreds of spices, teas, and coffees from around the world.

BROILED HALIBUT WITH CUCUMBER-DILL CREAM

A cool, creamy cucumber sauce laced with dill makes a classic accompaniment to simply prepared fish, such as halibut. Nicknamed the "hippo of the sea," the halibut is the largest of all flatfish. It is considered one of the finest of Northwest seafoods, for its delicately flavored, lean white flesh cooks up tender and large-flaked.

1½ pounds halibut fillets, bones removed, rinsed, drained, patted dry, and cut into 4 pieces (6 ounces each)

2 tablespoons freshly squeezed lemon juice
Kosher or sea salt
Freshly ground black pepper

1. Make the Cucumber-Dill Cream, allowing at least 1 hour preparation time. To prepare the halibut, 10 minutes before cooking, preheat the broiler. Lightly coat a baking sheet with oil or nonstick cooking spray.

2. Sprinkle flesh side of each fish fillet with 1½ teaspoons of the lemon juice and salt and pepper to taste, and arrange skin side down on baking sheet without crowding. Place fish under broiler 3 to 4 inches from heat source, and cook about 10 minutes per inch of thickness without turning, or until fillets just turn opaque.

3. To serve, place halibut fillets on individual plates and top with a dollop of Cucumber-Dill Cream. Pass remaining sauce at the table.

Serves 4

CUCUMBER-DILL CREAM

¾ cup peeled, seeded, diced cucumber
¼ teaspoon kosher salt
½ cup plain nonfat, lowfat, or regular yogurt
½ cup nonfat, lowfat, or regular sour cream

1 tablespoon fresh snipped dill or 1 teaspoon dried dill, crumbled
1 teaspoon freshly squeezed lemon juice
⅛ teaspoon freshly ground white pepper

1. Place cucumbers in a small sieve over a bowl, sprinkle with kosher salt, and toss to coat well. Set cucumbers aside at room temperature for 30 minutes to drain.

2. In a medium bowl, combine cucumbers, yogurt, sour cream, dill, lemon juice, and pepper. Mix well, cover, and refrigerate at least 30 minutes or as long as overnight to allow flavors to blend.

Makes 1½ cups sauce

A pewter teapot hanging from a wooden sign signals the Post Alley entrance to a world of workhorse and whimsical teapots. From England comes Sadler's reliable if homely Brown Betty, a basic teapot for everyday use. Cast-iron pots in classic designs hail from Japan, where they have been used for centuries in traditional tea ceremonies. Luxurious blue-and-gilt Lomonosov porcelain teapots are collector's items first manufactured in 1744 in St. Petersburg for the czar and his court. Yixing teapots from China, handmade vessels cast of porous purple clay found near Shanghai and first produced during the Ming dynasty, are yet another option.

In addition to teapots, the **Perennial Tea Room's** owners, Sue Zuege and Julee Rosanoff, carry all the accessories to go along with proper tea taking—tea strainers, cozies, sugar-and-cream sets, linen tea towels, toast racks, trays, and electric kettles. A black, green, herbal, flavored, and bergamot tea are brewed each day for customers to sample or to enjoy by the cup or by the pot. A selection of more than sixty teas in bulk provide numerous choices for the perfect "cuppa."

Proteus blossoms rise up like earthbound sea anemones. Venus's-flytraps and pitcher plants wait patiently to entrap the passing mite or fruit fly. The air is slightly humid, redolent with the odor of damp earth.

The rarefied atmosphere is a perfect haven for the exotic orchids, insectivorous plants, unusual cacti, and flowering species that the store has specialized in since it opened in 1979. Many grow in pots. "Air plants," like the bromeliad, take their nourishment from the air and rain and often grow on companion plants. Still others, such as the birds of paradise in vivid shades of yellow, blue, and red, or the tiny Dendrobium orchids in purple or white, are available by the stem, flown in several times a week from Hawaii and other tropical isles.

You'll often see Sarah Clementson Yaeger, a pretty, red-haired artist, toting an easel and paint box around Pike Place in search of her latest inspiration. Since 1981, Sarah has been creating "watercolors fresh daily," scenes of the Market that she sells at **Studio Solstone** with the help of her husband, Michael Yaeger.

Michael is a Falstaffian figure with a full head of gray hair and a curly beard. He runs the studio; acts as copywriter and graphic designer for the posters, notecards, and annual calendars made from Sarah's art; and self-publishes fiction and nonfiction books. He is affectionately

Right: About a third of the Market's one-hundred-plus farmers are Lao Highland families who sell year-round.

known as the "unofficial mayor of the Market" for his candid opinions and insider's knowledge.

Cigar aficionados seek out **Market Tobacco Patch** for the freshest cigars and a wide selection of special cutting devices and lighters that go along with the cigar-smoking ritual. Co-owner Murad Baluch personally tests each kind of cigar he sells so he can assist customers. The walk-in, twenty-two-foot humidor, with its carefully controlled environment (70° Fahrenheit and 70 percent humidity), occupies an entire wall. Cigar fanciers can choose among three hundred different types of cigars with fanciful names such as the Playboy, the Gran Corona, or the Churchill.

Milagros Mexican Folk Art & Handicrafts may be the Market's most colorful shop, with

Left: A produce vendor dressed for the cold, damp Northwest weather.

hand-painted dragons hanging from the ceiling, embroidered tapestries, tin luminaries, and a large selection of Día de los Muertos (Day of the Dead or All Souls' Day) skeleton figures. Religious wall hangings and crosses, animal-shaped candleholders, and hand-painted furniture are other examples of the artwork available here.

Left Bank Books specializes in alternative literature, magazines, posters, bumper stickers, Beat poetry, and music for activists, artists, and laborers. The anti-authoritarian bookstore has been in the Market for more than twenty-five years, but nobody owns the store. Rather, it is a seven-member collective in which decisions are made as a group with the store's ideals, rather than individual financial gain, in mind. Everyone is considered boss, manager, and worker; only the seven collective members are paid staff, and the store survives due to volunteer help.

The human-sounding chatter and unmistakable squawks and squeals of parrots, cockatiels, finches, parakeets, and other birds alert you to the Western Avenue location of the **Parrot Market,** which houses the largest selection of parrots in Washington State. Up to two hundred birds reside here on any given day, so a visit to the shop is more like a tour of the bird house at the zoo than an excursion to a retail store.

On permanent display are rare, not-for-sale birds, including Prince, the store mascot. With crimson wings and fluorescent green body, the parrot talks up a storm, waves, and even shakes hands with visitors. Anna, a Mexican red-headed Amazon whose cage perches right above the cash register, is another favorite of customers, especially when she whistles in their direction and greets them with "hello" and "goodbye."

All of the parrots are born domestically and raised from the egg. They are tame, hand-fed, healthy birds; none are imported or captured in the wild. Descriptive cards above each animal's cage provide background information—name, breed, hatch date, talking ability, diet information, general personality type for that particular breed, and cost. Prices range from $14 for the commonplace parakeet to almost $1,700 for the difficult-to-breed Moluccan cockatoo.

Men in White Coats

Inside the meat locker at **Don & Joe's Meats,** carcasses dangle headless and hoofless on sharp metal hooks. The heavy smell of curing meat mixes with the pungent scent of spices used to make fresh sausage. The air is chill.

Things are done much as they've always been here. Special orders are neatly arranged and tagged with the customer's name. The stainless steel sink, hamburger grinder, and work tables are spotless. Sawdust peppers the floor.

Outside, you'll find no plastic wrap, Styrofoam trays, or Cryovac packaging at the wraparound counter under the Market clock. As in the real meat markets of yesteryear, butchers in white coats and caps wrap your order in environmentally friendly butcher paper. Don & Joe's features a complete selection of beef, lamb, veal, pork, and poultry. The smoked hams, fresh turkeys, lamb chops, and stuffed pork chops are longtime favorites. Handmade Italian sausages, bratwurst, and Mexican chorizo—along with the newest addition, lamb sausages—are popular.

The shop also sells less traditional cuts, such as brains, sweetbreads, and lamb tongues. Turkey fillets and free-range chicken are available, as are geese, capons, and ducks. Owner Don Kuzaro Jr. and his crew take pride in filleting and boning to the customer's request and are willing to special-order almost any meat or fowl they don't stock.

It all started back in the 1960s, when Don Kuzaro Sr. and his brother-in-law, Joe Darby, worked together at Dan's Meat Market. The two men shared that all-American dream of one day owning the business. When Dan left the Market in 1969, Don and Joe were given first shot to buy the store, and Don & Joe's Meats was born.

Don Jr., who worked alongside his dad for many years, bought the business in the mid-1980s. He's a youthful man with a boyish smile and generous attitude. "I'm thankful I had a

The public toilets just down the stairs under the Market clock are known as the **South Publics,** and were the first public restroom facilities constructed by the City of Seattle, in 1908. Public facilities were more lavish in those days, and the South Publics boasted eight stalls for men and five for women, all adorned with marble panels and decorative tile.

Because of lengthy lines, the toilets were remodeled and the configuration switched in 1998, so that women got eight stalls and men five. As Paul Dunn, a Market resident and former chair of the Pike Place Market Historical Commission, commented, "These public restrooms are the most democratic services in the city. They serve the housed and the homeless, the resident and the tourist, the stable and the transient. As such, they truly reflect the essence of the Pike Place Market."

The city's second comfort station was built in 1910 under the sidewalks of Pioneer Square with even more lavish touches of marble and tile. Unfortunately, those stalls are closed, and all that remains is the ornate iron-and-glass pergola above ground.

chance to work with my dad, a friendly, honest, hardworking man, whom I've tried to be like in running my business," Don explains. "Also, my

Right: Looking east up Post Alley, where a half-block-long collage decorates the wall.

father-in-law, Curly Hanada, was a Market farmer, and I used to watch him sell and talk to his customers. They are both gone now, but not forgotten."

The Anonymous Gift

An appreciative crowd huddles before the tiny storefront window along Pike Place as Vladimir Kotelnikov prepares his latest batch of apple-cinnamon rolls. The tall man with the graying hair, mustache, and muscular arms stretches a round of dough until it forms a rough rectangle, sprinkles it with cinnamon sugar, tops it with apples and grated cheese, and then eases it into a long cylinder, jelly-roll fashion. He cuts the roll into inch-wide sections, turns them up like pinwheels, and places them on a baking sheet headed for the oven.

Steps away, Vladimir's wife, Zina, plucks a salmon piroshky from the display case and pops it into a white paper bag. The savory pastry is shaped like a fish and filled with smoked salmon pâté. A half dozen customers sit at the handful of stools set up inside, but the shop, called simply **Piroshky-Piroshky,** is so crowded that most take away their goodies to consume elsewhere. They might choose among artfully wrought piroshky, sweet pastries and coffee cakes, whole baked apples wrapped in puff pastry and filled

with sweet cream cheese, or Vladimir's *kringel,* a six-inch swirl of raisins, nuts, orange zest, and spices.

The Kotelnikovs are among the Market's great success stories. The couple and their two children immigrated from Estonia, where Vladimir was a baking instructor and Zina was an attorney.

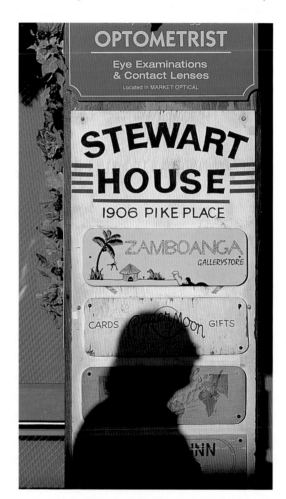

Left: Built in 1902, Stewart House predated the formation of the Market.

PERKY PEACH SALSA

Although the recipe specifies fresh peaches, you can use this simple salsa formula all year round with just about any ripe, sweet, fleshy fruit of your choice, from tropical fruits (papayas or mangos) to berries. The colorful confetti of a salsa that results is best enjoyed with fish, chicken, pork, or beef hot off the grill.

1 or 2 ripe peaches, about 8 ounces total, cored and coarsely chopped

1 jalapeño pepper, rinsed, seeds and membranes removed, coarsely chopped (see note)

1 green onion, root end and top 2 inches removed, remaining portion coarsely chopped

2 large or 4 small fresh mint leaves, coarsely chopped

2 teaspoons extra-virgin olive oil

4 teaspoons freshly squeezed lime juice

¼ teaspoon grated lime zest

Place all ingredients in a food processor and pulse just until a chunky sauce forms. Alternatively, dice all ingredients by hand and mix together. Place in a small bowl, cover, and allow salsa to sit at room temperature for ½ hour, or store in the refrigerator if not serving within ½ hour. Remove salsa from refrigerator ½ hour before serving.

Makes ¾ cup

Note: Jalapeños vary in hotness. Test by dabbing a small piece of cut pepper on the tip of your tongue. If very hot, add only half a pepper; if mild, use a whole pepper.

After settling in Seattle, Vladimir got a job at the Kaleenka Bakery in Redmond (sister operation to the Kaleenka restaurant in the Market), while his wife attended culinary school. When space in the Market became available, they borrowed money from neighbors in the Russian community to open a piroshky business.

In debt to the tune of $24,000 and with only $50 in his pocket, Vladimir hardly had enough money to buy the flour and butter to make enough pastries to open his shop. But the night before his new business was to open, somebody stuck an envelope containing $1,000 under the door. Vladimir later found out that the anonymous donor with the generous heart was the owner of the Kaleenka, who might have viewed the new venture as a competitor but apparently wished the Kotelnikovs nothing but success.

Food of the Gods

A few miles from the Market, a sweet chocolate cloud surrounds a squat, boxy building at Twenty-Third and East Cherry in Seattle's Central District. It's beat up around the edges and crowded, but homey, inside the factory where **Dilettante Chocolates** are produced.

Dana Taylor Davenport is the fifty-something master chocolatier, bigger-than-life personality, and guiding spirit behind Dilettante Chocolates. His chocolate factory "is not highly structured nor mechanically inclined." Indeed, most of the operations are performed by hand or on vintage equipment that belonged to his grandfather, Earl Remington Davenport, a chocolate maker and engineer. The hand extruder (circa 1910) turns out forty-eight truffle centers in each pressing, while the panning machine, a rotating copper kettle, coats nuts and coffee beans with chocolate.

The mostly female candymakers converse in their native Thai while they roll truffle centers with one hand and then dip them in tempered chocolate with the other. One woman puts the finishing touch—a dark chocolate X—on top of the Madame X truffles. These dark chocolate truffles are flavored with Pernod, a licorice-flavored French liqueur, and then coated in white chocolate.

Male workers use long wooden paddles to stir copper kettles bubbling with chocolate, butter, cream, and cocoa powder. Once reduced, the mixture becomes a premium chocolate sauce used by a leading Seattle coffee chain to flavor its mochas.

The humble factory belies Dilettante's royal roots, for the company traces its beginnings to the courts of Europe. At the turn of the twentieth century, Julius Rudolph Franzen served apprenticeships in Budapest and Paris before his commission in Vienna to Austria's Emperor Franz Josef. Later Julius became master candymaker to Czar Nicholas II in St. Petersburg. After immigrating to the United States in 1910, he shared the Old World formulas with his brother-in-law, Earl Davenport.

Today Dana Davenport, Earl's grandson, continues the family tradition with his master creations in chocolate. "I strive to make each individual piece in my chocolate collection the standard in its class," Dana says.

At the elegant Pike Place Market retail outlet, display cases are lined with truffles of every description. Dilettante's signature item, the Ephemere, is a creamy dark chocolate center enriched with butter, flavored with vanilla, and then dipped in either dark or milk chocolate. The Champagne Truffle Romanov, a semisweet chocolate center flavored with the essence of champagne and strawberry garni, is the customers' second-favorite selection. Women favor the Amaretto Truffle, while the Ephemere Mint Truffle is gaining ground among the gents in the crowd.

Right: A landing on the open-air stairwell between Western Avenue and Pike Place provides access to the Down-Under.

Tattoo You

JANET LIDDLE, A CONSULTING ARCHAEOLOGIST, AND HER DAUGHTER JAVILA HAVE made the trek from Ashford, Washington, to **Vyvyn's Tattoo.** For years, Javila has begged her mother for a tattoo, but since legal age in Washington State is eighteen, she's had to wait until today—her eighteenth birthday.

Javila, a pretty brunette in a baby-blue tank top, is stretched out on her stomach on a black examining table. Her right shoulder is exposed to Erika, the tattoo artist, a dark-haired woman with wire-rimmed glasses, punky-tipped hair, and a metal stud through her upper lip. The buzz of the tattoo machine comes in fits and starts like an angry insect as Erika fills in a line, then pauses to dip the needle into one of several tiny pots filled with inks in rainbow shades.

For the past two hours, the tattooist has been designing the young woman's dream tattoo—a delicate, colorful dragonfly with lacy wings. The skin is slightly raised and red where the ink goes in, but Javila doesn't even flinch. Both mother and daughter beam when they see the final result, about the size of a small fist.

"Just don't show it to Grandma," the mother warns her daughter as she writes out a check for $160, tax included.

Women and young people with tattoos are commonplace today, but when Vyvyn Lazonga (born Beverly Bean) got her first job as a tattoo artist in Seattle in 1972, the tattoo was a macho rite of passage. The male owner of the parlor billed her as the "Youngest Tattooist in the World." When she won the title of "World's Best Tattooed Female," he added that to her billing. Vyvyn vividly remembers the "dark ages," when sailors, soldiers, and tourists would come in to gawk at the three Japanese-style birds of paradise that adorn her torso.

Vyvyn started her own parlor in 1979 and eventually owned parlors in San Francisco and Seattle. Her tattoo parlor is nothing like most people's preconceived notion of a seedy room in

Left: After hours in the North Arcade belies the daily throng of shoppers.

PACIFIC RIM SEAFOOD BOIL

The Dungeness crab—*Cancer magister,* or the "big crab"—provides one of the best traditional foods of the region. Here the "Dungie" finds refuge in a light, healthy broth redolent with fresh lemongrass and gingerroot, a Pacific Rim twist on the traditional Northwest crab feed. To eat this dish properly, seafood forks, crab crackers, and extra napkins are mandatory.

1 tablespoon peanut oil

1 pound Alaskan spot prawns or medium-sized shrimp, shelled and deveined, shells reserved

4 stalks lemongrass, outer leaves discarded and soft inner core chopped into ¼-inch rounds, about ½ cup

2 tablespoons minced gingerroot

4 cloves garlic, halved

Pinch hot red pepper flakes

½ cup mirin (Japanese rice wine) or dry sherry

4 cups homemade vegetable stock or 2 cans (14½ ounces each) vegetable broth

1½ cups water

2 precooked 1- to 1½-pound Dungeness crabs in the shell, cracked into pieces suitable for picking

Pickled ginger, for garnish

1. Heat oil in a large wok or Dutch oven over medium heat. Add the shrimp shells (but not the shrimp), lemongrass, gingerroot, and garlic and cook 2 to 3 minutes, or until mixture is aromatic and shrimp shells turn opaque, stirring frequently. Add the pepper flakes, mirin, stock, and water and bring to a boil. Reduce heat, cover pan, and simmer 10 minutes. Remove broth from heat and pour through a fine-meshed strainer, pressing solids with a spoon to squeeze out all the juice. Discard solids.

2. Return broth to wok and bring to a gentle simmer. Add the prawns and cook 2 to 3 minutes, or until they just turn pink. With a slotted spoon, remove prawns to a bowl and reserve.

3. Add the crab pieces to the broth and cook 2 to 3 minutes, or until crab is warmed through, stirring occasionally. Return shrimp to the broth and remove from heat.

4. To serve, divide seafood and broth among individual bowls and garnish with pickled ginger.

Serves 4 as an entrée, 6 as an appetizer

a low-rent district frequented by Sailor Joes and bikers. At the storefront along Western Avenue, everything from eastern Zen to rollicking reggae music plays softly in the background. A soothing, incenselike smell wafts through the air. Oriental rugs, billowing drapes, and a statue of

Buddha decorate the waiting room. Vyvyn's art, from full-size canvases that brighten the walls to samples of tattoo designs in display cases, show that she is first and foremost an artist who just happens to use the human body as her canvas.

"In ancient and aboriginal societies, tattoos were applied to women to ensure that they would be able to endure the pain of childbearing. Among men, if one withstood the pain of a tattoo, he was considered to be a worthy warrior," Vyvyn explains thoughtfully as her forefinger traces the bold tribal tattoo that snakes over her hand and up her wrist.

But she advises prospective clients to "think before you ink, since you wear a tattoo design on your body forever. And if you can't take the pain, don't bother coming in. After all, there is something to be said for earning your art."

In the Beginning—Continued

Frank Goodwin was a character, a visionary, and a man ahead of his time. At the turn of the twentieth century, he made a fortune in the Klondike, produced a steam-propelled automobile that almost mowed down Theodore Roosevelt and his horse, and established Seattle's first gasoline service station. But he is best remembered as the realtor and self-taught architect who founded and designed the Pike Place Market.

By November 30, 1907, the privately held Goodwin Real Estate Company had completed the first pergola of the main arcades. The permanent shelter for farmers and other food shops extended from the Leland Hotel north along the bluff above Western Avenue. Farmers and gardeners selling their own produce were given first priority as tenants. On opening day, all seventy-six stalls were rented.

In this quasi-public venture, the city was involved in controls but never in ownership, which was left in the private hands of Frank and his family members, in the form of Goodwin Realty.

Daystalls, where farmers and artisans still sell today, rented for 10 cents a day. They were divided into the "dry" wood-topped tables, where eggs and dairy products were displayed, and the "wet" tables, covered with tin to allow for frequent sprinkling of vegetables. The farmers went on strike when several of the prime stalls were held out for the dreaded commission men to sell their produce, but Goodwin reasoned that commission produce was necessary when local producers stopped coming to the Market in the winter. Today, they're known as the highstalls.

The heyday of the Market came during the 1930s, with more than six hundred farmers issued permits to sell. During the Depression, the Market provided a welcoming environment to the city's jobless, as well as inexpensive food

Right: **The Corner Market building, with its arched windows, gabled roof line, and decorative brickwork, was built in 1912.**

HERBED CORN BREAD

The all-American favorite, corn bread, is updated here with the addition of sweet corn and herbs of the season. The flavor changes depending on the type of herb you use—sage lends a mellow, earthy taste; dill gives a bracing, piney flavor; and thyme has a sweet, pungent effect.

2 tablespoons unsalted butter	2 large eggs
1 cup all-purpose flour	1/2 cup lowfat buttermilk
1 cup yellow cornmeal	1 cup fresh or frozen corn kernels (thawed if frozen)
1 tablespoon sugar	1 tablespoon minced fresh dill, sage, or thyme
2 teaspoons baking powder	or 1 1/2 teaspoons dried dill, thyme, or oregano, crumbled
1/2 teaspoon baking soda	
1/4 teaspoon salt	

1. Preheat oven to 375°F. Place butter in a 9-inch pie plate or 9-inch ovenproof skillet and heat in oven for 5 minutes, or until butter melts. Do not allow butter to burn.

2. Meanwhile, in a mixing bowl, stir together the flour, cornmeal, sugar, baking powder, baking soda, and salt. In a separate bowl, beat eggs until frothy, then add buttermilk, corn, and herbs. Remove pie plate from oven and brush melted butter over bottom and sides. Pour extra butter into egg mixture and return pie plate to oven. Add wet ingredients to dry ingredients and stir until combined.

3. Carefully remove pie plate from oven, pour in batter and smooth top of dough, and immediately return to oven.

4. Bake for 20 to 25 minutes, or until top is lightly browned and a toothpick inserted in the center comes out with just a few crumbs. Loosen edges of corn bread, cut corn bread into 6 wedges, and serve immediately.

Serves 6

for the hungry. In 1941, Frank Goodwin sold out to Joe Desimone, who became president of Pike Place Markets, Inc., and proprietor of the Market. Although Joe died of a stroke in 1946, the Desimone family continued to run the Market until 1971.

The year 1941 was also the last harvest for Japanese-American farmers at Pike Place. It has been estimated that two-thirds of the 513 farmers selling in 1941 were Japanese Americans. Those impressive numbers changed almost overnight when Executive Order 9066, signed by President Roosevelt on February 19, 1942, called for internment of all Japanese Americans, even Nisei (second-generation children born in America), living in sensitive military areas such as Western Washington.

Japanese farmers were forced to dispose of personal property, were relocated to "Camp Harmony" in Puyallup, Washington, and were later transported to permanent internment camps for the duration of World War II. Banners in the Market proudly proclaimed the new "All-American Farmers' Row." More than one-third of the evacuated Japanese never returned to Seattle. In addition, many farmers went to work in defense plants, acres of prime farmland were paved over by industry, people moved to the suburbs, and the local supermarket became an accepted convenience. By 1949, the number of farmer-vendor licenses had declined to 53.

By the early 1950s, the pedestrian bridge linking the Market to the waterfront had been removed, and rerouting of public transportation made the intersection at First and Pike less important. The Market buildings slowly deteriorated as Seattle's dedication dried up.

Nevertheless, a few businesses thrived, some hardy farmers hung on, and the neighborhood refused to die. In 1954, Frank Goodwin passed on at the ripe old age of 89.

If the Shoe Fits

Walter DeMarsh's storefront along Western Avenue is a long, narrow space with concrete walls, exposed lightbulbs, and low ceilings. Tanned hides in autumn-leaf colors hang from hooks along the walls. Wooden lasts in odd sizes and shapes tangle together on floor-to-ceiling shelves. Half-finished shoes litter an old pedal-operated sewing machine. The air smells of machine oil, leather pelts, and dust.

Mobeta Shoes is like a shoemaker's shop plucked from the Middle Ages, and Walter only adds to the medieval ambiance with his graying beard, long hair braided and tied with a black ribbon, and dark beret. Well-worn jeans are tucked into two-toned leather boots that rise to his knees. He discovered his life's calling, making shoes for people with difficult-to-fit feet, as the result of a motorcycle accident in his youth that left him with one leg $2\frac{1}{2}$ inches shorter than the other.

After spending an agonizing two years in a cast and then breaking his leg a second time due to ill-fitting shoes, Walter met Heinz Heiss. The Seattle shoemaker constructed a comfortable, form-fitting boot for Walter, and a year later the young man began an apprenticeship with Heiss that lasted two years. Walter opened his store on Western Avenue in 1978, but he didn't even put up a sign until 1993, when he was sure he had learned his craft.

The work at Mobeta Shoes is slow and exacting because each shoe is crafted from the ground up. Walter takes tracings of his clients' feet, shapes wooden forms that match the tracings, then builds shoes and a leather-and-cork insert around the forms. Customers, including people who have been injured, had polio, or simply have mismatched feet, are an important part of the process. "Making the shoe is easy. Making it fit is hard. I'm not a magician or a mind reader, and supplying a handmade product to the person with unique feet requires the customer's commitment and participation as well as my own," Walter explains. Once the shoemaker has a good fit, he tries to make the shoes less orthopedic-looking and more fashionable—no easy task when feet are curved like half moons or as wide as bear paws. But if push comes to shove, fit overcomes appearance every time.

Since Walter works alone and there are only so many hours in the day, he produces only about forty pairs of shoes a year. Not even Walter can cobble time.

Left: Walter DeMarsh, owner of Mobeta Shoes, crafts footwear the old-fashioned way.

Right: A reflection of the Corner Market building.

One of the Market Foundation's special projects is the **Pike Place Market Heritage Center.** Located on Western Avenue and the first stop on many visitors' agendas, the Heritage Center uses exhibits, interactive computer kiosks, historical photographs and videos, architectural pieces, artifacts, and maps to help educate the public about the Market's history, diverse population, and ties to the region's agriculture, immigration, urban development, and civic life. The center presents the Market as a diverse, vibrant, and evolving part of Seattle's past, present, and future.

Short on Top, Long on Memories

The "memory window" at **Trudy & Lenora's** is a glass scrapbook back in time. A pair of faded photos behind the barbershop's plate glass windows shows present owner Viola Brown's mother, Lenora, cutting the same man's hair—fifty years apart.

Three generations of lady barbers in Viola's family have clipped Seattleites' hair at this Market fixture in Stewart House. The legacy started with Helen Sullivan, Viola's grandmother, who started cutting hair at Third and James and refused to move even as workers demolished the building around her. Only the threat of rain and a new lease in the Public Market convinced her to move her shop in the 1920s. During the Depression, hobos painted an X onto the shop's doorjamb, a signal among the homeless that Helen was an easy touch. She gave them handouts and spare change; saved old, half-smoked cigarettes for the indigent; and bought them neckties at rummage sales.

Helen's daughter Lenora became a barber and worked with her mother, although their relationship was so stormy that they had to subdivide the shop. The feud reached unimaginable proportions when Lenora left for a weekend and came back to find the shop painted purple, a color she detested. The next time Helen left town, Lenora repainted the shop blue. One day when Lenora was gone, Helen installed purple sinks. Mother bested daughter in that feud, because there was no getting rid of the sinks.

Today, the portly woman barber in her white smock and half glasses works alone in a peaceful atmosphere. You get not only a cut but a consultation each time you visit Viola, who often guesses her customers' ancestry by their skin and hair type and has an uncanny ability to detect oncoming illnesses. Longtime customers appreciate such highly personal service along with the inexpensive prices Viola charges.

More than two hundred artists and craftspeople sell at the Market.

The Foundation of the Market

Few visitors to the Market realize that five social service agencies are located within its nine acres. **Pike Market Medical Clinic, Downtown Food Bank, Pike Market Senior Center, Heritage House at the Market,** and **Pike Market Child Care & Preschool** are administered by the Market Foundation, whose mission is "to preserve the traditions and diversity of the Pike Place Market community." It's a fragile community, with close to five hundred low-income people living in the Market itself and nearly ten thousand low-income and elderly people living within a one-mile radius.

Food, hot meals, health care, shelter, child care, emergency groceries, companionship, and employment and housing assistance are routinely available to those in need. This sets Pike Place apart, since no other public market in the United States provides low-income housing or services to its residents. The Market Foundation fulfills its mission with the help of the Pike Place Market Preservation and Development Authority (PDA) and by raising private funds.

Right: Demetrios Moraitis, owner of Mr. D's Greek Delicacies, entertains passersby with his *bouzouki,* a Greek mandolin.

The foundation contributes to many special projects, including Market Fresh, a "food stamp" program that enables participants to redeem coupons for fresh produce from the Market's farm tables. The volunteers at FoodLink collect twenty thousand pounds of food from Market farmers and vendors each year for redistribution to downtown food banks and meal programs. The foundation also sponsors a resident advocate, a social worker who helps neighborhood residents secure social and health services.

Good Karma

The lighting is dim, dark floorboards creak underfoot, and incense burns fitfully at **Tenzing Momo & Co.,** one of the first herbal apothecaries on the West Coast when it opened back in 1977. It's an atmospheric place, modeled after a Tibetan pharmacy, where the focus is decidedly more Old Age than New Age.

Co-owner Eric Pollard and his staff of trained herbalists dispense their remedies along with brewing and dosage instructions, lots of positive encouragement, and a sense of caring.

Left: Balloon art is raised to a high level in the Market.

SPICY RED MUSSELS

Because they taste like a cross between an oyster and a clam, mussels are often referred to as the "poor man's oyster." Found the world over, mussels are plentiful, inexpensive, versatile, and easy to cook. The Northwest's own Penn Cove and Mediterranean mussels are especially appealing.

2 pounds mussels, scrubbed and debearded just before cooking

½ cup dry white wine or water

2 bay leaves

2 tablespoons extra-virgin olive oil

¼ cup minced shallots

1 teaspoon minced jalapeño pepper or ½ teaspoon hot red pepper flakes, crumbled

2 cloves garlic, minced

½ cup minced plum tomatoes

¼ cup firmly packed unseasoned soft bread crumbs (see note)

2 tablespoons freshly grated Parmigiano-Reggiano or Parmesan cheese

¼ cup minced flat-leaf parsley, plus extra parsley sprigs for garnish

1. In a large stockpot or Dutch oven with a lid, combine mussels, water, and bay leaves. Bring to a boil over medium-high heat, cover, and cook 5 to 7 minutes, or until mussels open. Shake pan occasionally during cooking to redistribute mussels. With a slotted spoon, remove mussels that have opened, and continue cooking remaining mussels 1 to 2 minutes longer. Remove open mussels and discard any that do not open.

2. If desired, strain mussel liquid through several thicknesses of dampened cheesecloth and save for use in another recipe. When mussels are cool enough to handle, remove meat from shells and reserve. Break each shell into two half shells and save a fourth of the shells, choosing the largest and most attractive ones. Evenly space shells on a baking sheet, and arrange two mussels in each half shell. Set aside baking sheet while preparing the filling. Preheat the broiler and arrange the oven rack so that it is 3 to 4 inches from the heat source.

3. In a medium skillet, heat olive oil over medium-high heat. Add shallots, jalapeño, and garlic, and cook 1 to 2 minutes, stirring constantly. Remove pan from heat and stir in tomatoes, bread crumbs, cheese, and parsley. Divide stuffing among mussels, pressing down so that it forms a layer over the shellfish. Broil 2 to 4 minutes, or until the filling is warmed through and lightly browned.

4. To serve, place mussels on a large platter or divide among individual plates. Garnish with parsley sprigs.

Serves 8 to 12 as an appetizer

Note: To make unseasoned soft bread crumbs, tear a slice of white or whole wheat bread into chunks, place in a food processor, and process until crumbs form.

Belly up to the counter in the open air and devour half a cracked Dungeness crab or a bowl of cioppino at **Jack's Fish Spot**. Since 1982, owner Jack Mathers has been in the Market, where his business stands apart as the only fish stand with fresh seafood tanks, a seafood-smoking facility, and a small seafood bar. The seafood bar serves smoky clam chowder, steamed clams, oysters on the half shell, and fried seafood seven days a week. A narrow lunch counter with a handful of coveted stools is a fun perch from which to watch the staff cook up your choice of seafood—cod, halibut, prawns, oysters, or scallops—fried in thin, crisp beer batter. The accompanying chips are hot, skin-on French-fried potatoes. Prices are cheap.

They start the process by chatting with their customers to gauge symptoms. Next they scoop dried herbs and flowers from the antique jars that line the back wall of the shop, weigh the dried ingredients on an old-fashioned brass scale, and then mix them in exacting proportions, creating plant-based alternatives that help people stay well through the use of herbs.

Tenzing Momo features the largest selection of dried herbs and flowers on the West Coast, and Eric is committed to finding as many locally and organically grown sources as he can, although his one hundred suppliers are sprinkled all over the globe. He describes his life's work as "good, guerrilla herbalism, since few places in the country offer trained herbalists in downtown locations. We're here for the people."

Some customers who are pressed for time head for the 370 premixed tinctures that line a lofty cabinet and are alphabetized by name—burdock root, detox formula, echinacea, milk thistle seed, St. John's wort. Others choose among three hundred essential oils that can heal the skin, act as an antidepressant, or simply create certain moods with their pleasing aromas. Many browse the floor-to-ceiling bookcases that boast more than five hundred volumes of herbology theories from around the world. Most days, a tarot card reader, palm reader, or Chief Thundercloud, the resident Native American psychic and shaman, gives readings, only adding to the strong, positive karma of Tenzing Momo.

A Fish Tale

City Fish lays claim to the most intriguing fish tale in the Market. It was started by the Seattle City Council in 1918 when the price of salmon skyrocketed to a whopping 25 cents a pound.

Hatchery-raised fish were brought in to compete against wholesale fish with great success, and city intervention helped bring the price of salmon down to just 10 cents a pound. Nonetheless, the city decided to bail out after several years of marginal profits.

David Levy, nicknamed "Good Weight Dave" by his appreciative customers because he didn't let his fingers linger on the scale, bought the business in 1922 and turned it into a Market institution symbolized by the bright neon fish

atop its roof. It was always a family-run enterprise; at one time, five Isaac Levys worked there. Market regulars used to enjoy calling out, "Hey, Isaac!" and watching five heads turn in their direction. Dave's descendants continued to run City Fish until 1995, when former Alaska fisherman Jon Daniels took over.

The "new kid" (relatively speaking) on the Pike Place Market fishmongers' block is a strapping young man with eyes as blue-gray as the surf and a viselike handshake forged by years at sea. Jon's hands-on experience in Alaska included time aboard a factory trawler, a long-liner, and his father's tender ship. In the off-season, he sold smoked seafood at shopping mall kiosks, learning sales techniques and customer service.

Since buying his own business, Jon has learned firsthand the unrelenting routine of owning a fish market. He's up at five-thirty every morning to begin the flurry of phone calls, paperwork, fish brokering, and trips to the airport that often lasts until nine o'clock at night. The hectic pace keeps up seven days a week, and life's a constant go, go, go. But his instinct for quality seafood, combined with excellent contacts within the fishing community and an abundance of youthful energy, bode well for Jon Daniels as he charts the course of City Fish.

Left: With a fiddle, tambourine, cymbal, cow and jingle bells, clapping coconut, and flapping duck wings, Greg Youmans treats onlookers to a one-man-band show.

FARMERS' MARKET VEGETABLE PUFF

This vegetarian entrée is closely related to the Dutch baby, a puffy pancake cooked in a skillet in the oven. Although usually served for breakfast with a sweet lemon sauce, the pancake turns savory in this rendition, with the addition of roasted vegetables of the season and Oregon Blue, an artisanal cow's milk cheese from the lush pastures of Oregon's Rogue River Valley Creamery.

1 pound small new potatoes (1 to 1½ inches in diameter), scrubbed and cut in half

½ pound asparagus or sugar snap peas, rinsed, patted dry, and trimmed

½ pound baby carrots, peeled

1 tablespoon extra-virgin olive oil

1 tablespoon balsamic vinegar

Kosher or sea salt and freshly ground black pepper

1 tablespoon butter

¾ cup lowfat milk

⅓ cup all-purpose flour

Pinch freshly ground white pepper

4 eggs or 1 cup egg substitute

2 ounces Oregon Blue cheese or other high-quality blue cheese, crumbled

Several sprigs of fresh herbs of the season, such as chives, basil, oregano, or thyme

1. Preheat oven to 475°F. To roast vegetables, lightly oil a baking sheet and arrange potatoes, asparagus, and carrots in a single layer without crowding. Drizzle vegetables with olive oil and balsamic vinegar. Sprinkle with salt and pepper and roast for 12 to 15 minutes, or until vegetables are tender and slightly charred, turning vegetables once or twice during cooking. Remove from oven and allow vegetables to cool on baking sheet.

2. To prepare vegetable puff, preheat oven to 400°F. Melt butter in a 9- or 10-inch nonstick, ovenproof skillet in oven until sizzling. Watch carefully, so butter does not burn.

3. Meanwhile, place milk, flour, and pepper in food processor or blender and pulse until blended. Add eggs and process just until blended.

4. Remove skillet from oven and immediately pour in egg batter. Bake, uncovered, in center of oven 15 to 18 minutes, until the pancake puffs and browns lightly. Do not open oven door while baking, or pancake could fall.

5. Remove puff from oven and sprinkle evenly with blue cheese. Cut into 2 or 4 wedges.

6. To serve, place wedges on individual plates and arrange roasted vegetables over wedges in an attractive pattern. Using clean kitchen scissors, snip herbs over wedges and serve immediately.

Serves 2 as an entrée, 4 as an appetizer

Music in the Air

The cacophony of sounds—dulcimer music, folk songs, a high-pitched flute—is one of the Market's ineffable charms. Within its boundaries, musicians, street performers, and balloon artists who perform in the open air are a very visible and vocal population. Anyone who wants to play music, sing, or entertain can

buy a permit from the Pike Place Market Preservation and Development Authority for $15 per calendar year.

About 160 permits are issued annually, and performers are considered another form of Market "producer," just like the farmers and craftspeople. However, unlike the latter populations, they are not screened before appearing. They must carry an instrument, but not necessarily a tune, so the advice is always "caveat listener."

The performers are allowed to play at fourteen spots within the Market, signified by red musical notes painted on the sidewalks and tiles. A number is also painted within each musical note, designating the number of performers who can play at that spot. A musician is allowed to perform for only one hour per spot; this is to keep the music from becoming too loud or monotonous to those residents who live above.

Jeanne Towne, a blind folksinger, has performed in the Market since 1976. Often she sets her stool outside Starbucks, a coveted musician spot because of the constant flood of foot traffic. She perches her version of a tip box, a wicker fishing creel, at her feet. With her bronzed face turned toward the sun, she strums her autoharp or guitar and sings happy tunes.

Meanwhile, members of a pan flute group from South America have chosen "the cave" for their musical performance. This is another prime

Right: Performers are considered another form of Market producer, just like the farmers and craftspeople.

Left: One of the many entrances to the Market, a stairway between Western Avenue and Pike Place.

spot, particularly for those playing in large groups, because of its reverberating acoustics, rather like a natural echo chamber. It's located in the open-air stairwell two levels below Rachel the Pig, and the overhanging mezzanine is often crowded with passersby who look on appreciatively.

Shaken, Not Stirred

As the sun sets and the jewel tones of twilight overtake Puget Sound, a plate of chicken *taquitos* with a glass of sangría at **Copacabana Cafe** is a great way to welcome the night. Climb the twisting circular staircase to the cafe's second-story location in the funky Triangle Building to discover Seattle's only Bolivian restaurant and one of the best sun decks in town.

The restaurant was established in the Sanitary Market in 1964 by Don Ramón and Hortensia Peláez, political exiles from Bolivia, and moved to its present location in 1978. Throughout the years, Copacabana has remained family-run, offering the same treasured recipes developed by the founders. Homestyle dishes such as paella (rice cooked in a saffron sauce with chicken, pork, shrimp, sausages, clams, mussels, and green peas), *salteña* (a meat and vegetable pie filled with potatoes, peas, carrots, and beef), and *sopa de camarones* (a highly spiced shrimp soup with potatoes and green peas) fill the menu. Traditional

desserts such as flan (caramel custard) and *arroz con leche* (rice pudding) make sweet endings. Beer, wine, sangría, or soft drinks imported from South America are options for sipping.

Many regulars down a plate of oysters on the half shell and a Northwest microbrew at **Emmett Watson's Oyster Bar** before heading home. Tucked back in the Soames-Dunn Building, Emmett Watson's is named for one of Seattle's most crusty, opinionated, oyster-lovin' journalists. Indeed, Emmett's very first *Seattle Post-Intelligencer* column is framed on one wall.

Everyone from the suits and silk dresses crowd to the T-shirt and tattoo contingent has been coming here since 1976 for the oysters on the half shell, true cod fish-and-chips, hand-cut French fries, and Puget Sound salmon soup (garlicky clam stock afloat with velvety strips of salmon and a crouton swabbed with aioli). Wine by the glass and bottle, half a dozen beers on tap, and almost twenty beers in bottles wash it all down.

The cornflower-blue booths and blue-and-white checked tablecloths are cozy and familiar. The menu is no fancier than hand-scrawled selections printed on brown paper bags. The waitstaff is laid-back and the place oozes scrappy charm, a true taste of Seattle.

Because of these attributes, in 1998 the James Beard Foundation, a nonprofit organization that

promotes appreciation of American food and wine, honored Emmett Watson's with its America's Regional Classics award. This honor is presented to "timeless, grassroots restaurants that serve memorable food and are strongly embedded in the fabric of their communities."

In the heart of the Main Arcade, twenty-eight stairs link the first, second, and third floors of **Lowell's Restaurant & Bar,** and on each level you will encounter a different dining experience. Many Market workers and insiders choose to have a bite or sip a drink on the restaurant's second floor, where half a dozen wooden booths project over the Main Arcade. Like the crow's nest of a ship, it's a great people-watching area for those who wish to peruse the passing floor show. The checkered linoleum floor, leather-and-chrome stools, and green Formica tabletops on the ground level give this portion of Lowell's the feel of a classic diner stashed in the steerage compartment of a ship. Alternatively, you can make the journey to level three, where floor-to-ceiling windows magnify the panoramic view of ferryboats, the Olympic Mountains, and container barges plying Puget Sound. No matter which experience you choose, Lowell's is known for its classic American fare—good, simple food at reasonable prices. It has been around since 1908, when Edward and William Manning spent $1,900 to open Manning's Coffee House. The

original grew into a chain of forty-six restaurants up and down the West Coast. The name changed to Lowell's in 1957, when Reid Lowell, one of its managers, acquired the Market location.

The Hotel Livingston, known for its "Modern Special Rates and Grand Sound Views," was built in 1901 at the corner of First and Virginia for seamen and longshoremen, who rented rooms by the week or the month. On this busy corner, just below the Livingston, the **Virginia Inn** was established in 1903. Today, the worn tiles on the floor attest to the bar's almost hundred-year history and great popularity through the decades. Here people of all ages and classes—tourists, business people, the young, and the not-so-young from the senior citizens' housing in the former hotel upstairs—mingle comfortably while knocking back a mixed drink, a single-malt Scotch, a glass of wine, or one of a dozen Northwest microbrews on tap. The menu ranges from hearty soups to Northwest-style crab cakes, and outside seating is popular at the venerable Virginia.

The Bees' Knees

The sun has set, and Doris and Don Mech are loading beehives into the back of their old flatbed truck. It's a 1979 model, and sometimes the elderly couple wonders just how much

Left: The Washington Mutual Tower dominates the skyline looking south along Pike Place.

STRAWBERRY-RHUBARB FOOL

The appearance of hothouse rhubarb in the highstalls is the first sign of spring in the Market. Weeks later, when the farmers bring in rhubarb fresh from the fields, it's proof that the crops are awakening after the long, rainy winter. Either type of rhubarb works well in this creamy "fool," an English dessert of puréed fruit (traditionally gooseberries) and whipped cream.

1 cup lowfat vanilla yogurt

2 pints strawberries, rinsed, patted dry, and hulled

3 stalks rhubarb, about ¾ pound, stem end and top ½ inch removed, rinsed, patted dry, and coarsely chopped

4 to 6 tablespoons Mount Rainier fireweed honey (or other mild-flavored honey)

1 cup whipping cream

Fresh mint sprigs, for garnish

1. Spoon yogurt into a fine-meshed sieve placed over a bowl and lined with a paper coffee filter or two thicknesses of dampened cheesecloth. Place in the refrigerator for 1 hour to drain. Coarsely chop 1 pint of the strawberries. Cut the remaining strawberries into halves if small, quarters if large.

2. Place the 1 pint of coarsely chopped strawberries and the rhubarb in a medium saucepan over medium-high heat. Cover and cook 5 to 7 minutes, or until fruit begins to lose its juice and bubble, stirring occasionally. Uncover pan, reduce heat, and simmer about 8 to 10 minutes, or until strawberries and rhubarb lose their shape and only a few lumps remain, stirring occasionally.

3. Add 4 tablespoons (¼ cup) of the honey and stir well to incorporate. Add the remaining pint of strawberries and cook over medium heat 3 to 5 minutes, stirring occasionally. The strawberries should be soft but still hold their shape. Taste and add 1 to 2 tablespoons more honey, if necessary. Pour mixture into a medium mixing bowl and allow to cool. Meanwhile, whip cream until stiff peaks form.

4. Add drained yogurt to strawberry-rhubarb mixture and stir well. Add whipped cream, folding in gently until only a few white streaks remain.

5. To serve, spoon strawberry mixture into individual dessert dishes or goblets. Garnish each with a sprig of fresh mint.

Serves 6 to 8

longer it can hold out, making journeys from **Mech Apiaries,** their honey farm in Maple Valley, Washington, to various sites around Puget Sound in search of fields of blossoming flowers —new sources of nectar for their honeybees.

Dressed in white outfits, their hands gloved and heads shielded in netting, the Mechs look like astronauts exploring the moon as they move the hives from ground level into the truck. The work is slow and exacting; each beehive contains two brood chambers where the queen bee is located. Each hive contains fifty thousand to sixty thousand bees. By the time they're ready to roll, the flatbed contains forty beehives swarming with more than two hundred thousand bees.

The Mechs move the hives to timberland owned by timber companies. They no longer use public lands, such as U.S. Forest Service property, because of senseless vandalism—people shooting heavy-gauge shotguns into the hives, running over the hives in big trucks, or simply pushing them over.

A few days before the bees are to be moved, Don drives the route to make sure the rural roads are in service. He clears out any weeds or debris so the bees' new location is ready and waiting. Once nightfall comes, the Mechs drive the insects to their new home, catch a few hours of sleep in the truck, and eat a light breakfast, including gourmet coffee (this is

Seattle, after all!). At sunup, they unload the hives and the bees.

"Suddenly, the bees are in green pastures again," according to Doris. "They're excited because they've moved from a place where the nectar was dwindling to a place where the nectar is free-flowing. Sometimes it literally drips from the flowers. The scout bees go out and discover the new blossoms. Then they do a special dance in front of the hive to alert the worker bees, and within fifteen minutes they're out gathering nectar again."

Like other types of farming, bee farming is seasonal and depends heavily on the presence or absence of rain. The bees need warm, sunny days to do their work, so the season begins in May, when the bees gather nectar from the flowers of broadleaf maple trees in Maple Valley to produce a robust-tasting, aromatic honey. It continues through late summer, when Doris and Don move the bees to the Kittitas Valley, where the insects feast on strawberry clover to produce a mild, delicate product.

"The seasons pass so quickly. Flowers fade and summer turns to brisk autumn and on to winter's cold," Doris muses. "Still, we have with us the sweet fragrance of blossoms now gone. Each jar of golden honey is the essence of spring, or a warm reminder of summer flowers on sunny slopes near Mount Rainier. To the seasoned traveler and honey connoisseur, taking a small jar of honey home is like taking home a little part of the land itself."

The Man Who Saved the Market

Victor Steinbrueck Park guards the Market's north flank, at the bottom of the steep hill formed by Virginia Street. Locals stroll with their pooches on the grassy berms, office workers from nearby buildings drink in the fresh air, and tourists hold hands while watching the sun set over Elliott Bay. Many of those enjoying the park are unaware of Victor Steinbrueck's valiant crusade to save the Market more than twenty-five years ago and his historic role as the Market's greatest friend and champion.

Back in 1958, city planners began looking at the Market with a critical eye. They felt there was a higher and better use for the Market's prime city acreage and hoped to "modernize" the area. By the 1960s, the Central Association had devised a plan that called for the demolition of everything from Union to Lenora Street and First to Western Avenue for creation of a terraced garage, park, hotel, high-rise offices, and other "modern" amenities.

The news was a self-described "major catastrophe" in the life of Victor Steinbrueck, a University of Washington architecture professor and civic leader. During the summer of 1964, officers of Allied Arts of Seattle, a local arts support group, formed the grassroots Friends of the Market (FOM) organization to oppose the Central Association's plan, with Victor and attorney Robert Ashley named co-chairs. The Friends agreed that the Market needed the hammer and paintbrush, not the wrecking ball. As Victor would later say, "Tearing down the Market would be like replacing Grandmother with a chorus girl."

Yet proponents of the urban renewal plan to revitalize the Market's prime piece of real estate were strong and included city hall, downtown business interests, the city council, and the local media. They dubbed the Market the "Historic Skid Road."

By the end of the 1960s, shifting political and economic forces, shrinking farmer participation, and the appearance of artists' and crafters' works on the day tables signaled a changing Market texture. The neighborhood was rough, with taverns and "adult amusement centers" on almost every block, a large number of alcoholic street people, and the beginnings of gangs and drug dealing.

In 1971 the city signed a contract with the Department of Housing and Urban Development (HUD) to develop "Pike Plaza." Pike Plaza would have replaced the deteriorating

Right: A joyful moment in Victor Steinbrueck Park.

created a seven-acre historical district with urban renewal to be based upon renovation and historic preservation. The Pike Place Market remains the only historical district in the nation created by citizen vote.

The Market Lifestyle

In 1984 Sharron and Robert Shinbo and their seventeen-year-old daughter, Roberta, sat down at the dining room table in their small 1920s bungalow in Montlake, a pleasant neighborhood about five miles from downtown Seattle. Each knew it was time to move to a new home, and each had a different prerequisite. Roberta wanted to live downtown; Sharron wanted a view; and Robert wanted to live within walking distance of his landscape architecture practice just north of the Market.

When the couple learned of a 950-square-foot condominium with a westerly view for sale in the Market, they didn't hesitate. When an office condominium in the same building became available, they bought that, too. By 1985, the Pike & Virginia building had become the Shinbos' home base and office space for Robert and his staff.

Although the physical structure of the Market was much the same then as it is now, the atmosphere was quite different. "Back then, you could

Market with a hotel, a thirty-two-story apartment house, four twenty-eight-story office buildings, a hockey arena, and a four-thousand-car parking garage.

The HUD-sponsored urban renewal schemes galvanized Victor Steinbrueck and the FOM. Its members gathered more than twenty-five thousand signatures to put a "Save the Market" initiative on the November 1971 ballot, one of the first such initiatives in Washington State. Seattle voters passed the initiative by a three-to-two ratio. In place of the HUD plan, the initiative

Left: The world-famous neon coffee cup outside Seattle's Best Coffee.

find a parking place on the street or at surface parking lots," Robert reminisces. "Starbucks was just a small storefront, nothing like the multinational behemoth of today. In 1985 it was slim pickings for fresh, locally grown, year-round produce, other than at the highstalls. That's changed, with many local farmers bringing and selling their harvest here. Organically grown food has become a more prominent and welcome feature of the Market in the last decade. Last but not least, I don't think they threw the salmon back in 1985!"

Sharron adds, "Back in the mid-1980s, the Market was a quiet community that wasn't even open on Sundays. As the Market has grown into the region's largest attraction, the number and diversity of people who come here have increased dramatically. Now, nine million people a year show up on our doorstep seven days a week."

Despite the rollicking atmosphere (indeed, perhaps because of it), Sharron and Robert are great proponents of the Market lifestyle.

Robert muses, "The Market is a microcosm—a city within a city. There are times, whole days and weekends, when we don't set foot (or drive) outside the Market. Besides fresh food, there is a small hardware store, over seventy restaurants, day care, medical clinic, food bank, money bank, clothing, kitchen supply stores, optometrist, a park, condom shop, and about five bookstores. Within a five-minute walk we can also go to the

art museum, symphony, aquarium, numerous galleries, athletic club, or the region's best department stores. Except for the funeral parlor—which has been replaced by a restaurant—everything you might want in this life or the hereafter is within a three-block walk of our home."

Très Français

Visitors passing through the brick-lined, flower-filled Inn at the Market courtyard take pleasure in observing a bevy of white-coated chefs chopping herbs, making sauces, and plating entrées

From 1941 until 1951, the Market housed an upscale bordello. Seattle's last big-time madam, **Nellie Curtis,** bought the old Outlook Hotel (circa 1909), located just south of the famous Public Market Center sign and Market clock, and rechristened it the LaSalle Hotel to sound more refined and exotic. Her girls distributed discreet calling cards along the waterfront reading "You are but a stranger once at Nellie's" and "Friends Easily Made." Today, the LaSalle Hotel plays a decidedly more humanitarian role. Transformed into the LaSalle Apartments, it provides forty-eight units of low-income housing for the Market's elderly population.

in the glass-enclosed exhibition kitchen at **Campagne.** This French country–style restaurant, whose name translates as "countryside," perches on the hillside along Pine Street, overlooking Pike Place and the working waterfront.

The dining room is simple yet elegant. Pale tan walls and low lighting from wall sconces, verdigris chandeliers, and flickering votive candles flatter all who enter. White tablecloths, fresh flowers, and French art posters set the mood.

The menu features a choice of two seasonal tasting menus, a French country–style family dinner Sunday through Wednesday, and à la carte selections that include country-style pork and chicken-liver pâté, horseradish-encrusted rack of lamb, grilled sea scallops served in a lobster and fennel broth, and saddle of rabbit stuffed with escarole and bacon. A cheese platter, chocolate hazelnut terrine, or warm almond and blueberry torte with lavender ice cream make fitting finales.

Café Campagne offers a less formal, less expensive alternative to its sister restaurant. At breakfast, house-baked baguettes and foamy

PEAR VINAIGRETTE

This silky, golden, sweet-tart dressing captures the simple fresh goodness of pears from the Northwest. I like it tossed with Bibb lettuce or spinach, quartered cremini or button mushrooms, and a handful of toasted hazelnuts.

1 ripe Comice or Bartlett pear, peeled, cored, and coarsely chopped	½ cup apple cider vinegar
1 tablespoon grated white or yellow onion	1 teaspoon Dijon mustard
¼ cup honey	¼ teaspoon Tabasco sauce
½ teaspoon kosher or sea salt	2 tablespoons hazelnut or walnut oil
	3 tablespoons canola or vegetable oil

In a food processor or blender, pulse pear, onion, honey, salt, vinegar, mustard, and Tabasco until smooth. Add hazelnut oil and canola oil and pulse until mixture thickens slightly. Use immediately or cover and refrigerate for up to 1 week.

Makes 1⅔ cups

lattes encourage you to linger over the morning newspaper. By lunchtime, the aioli-swabbed lamb burger with balsamic grilled onions and fire-roasted peppers, a perfectly prepared omelet, or salade niçoise might strike the proper chord. Steak frites, bouillabaisse, or roasted chicken redolent with *herbes de Provence* are favored dinner choices. Butter-colored walls, low ceilings, a long wooden banquette, and classical and jazz music set the mood, while strategically placed mirrors allow all patrons to see and be seen.

Rooms with a View

One of the charms of the Market is its physical setting. It was once lyrically described as "a cluster of buildings on a cliff above an inland sea." Today, many of the Market's restaurants and businesses take full advantage of the million-dollar views.

On a cold winter's day, with a storm blowing in off Puget Sound, there's no better place to witness nature's drama than from the cosseted confines of **Place Pigalle.** In the distance, gray clouds gather and angry sheets of rain pelt the turbulent waters of Elliott Bay. Inside, a periwinkle blue ceiling hovers above, white and black tiles checker the floor, and sophisticated paintings grace the walls. The cozy dark-wood bar specializes in premium and unusual spirits—French and

Swiss eaux-de-vie, Armagnac, and chilled aquavit and vodka.

Menus that change with the season reflect the bounty of the Northwest, mingling classic French, Mediterranean, and Asian influences. Northwest seafood, rabbit and other game, and classic French desserts, such as crème brûlée and pot de crème, are featured items.

Right: Place Pigalle restaurant is one of the many Market businesses that command a sweeping view of Puget Sound.

Just south of Place Pigalle, the dark green walls, French country tables and chairs, and fresh flowers on the tables at **Maximilien** conjure up visions of a favorite Parisian bistro, but the picture-postcard views of Puget Sound and the Olympic Mountains are pure Northwest.

Country French is the focus of co-owners Axel Macé and Eric Francy (who also serves as chef). Both hail from France and are professionally trained in the cuisine of their homeland, while the waitstaff ensures an authentic Gallic spirit. Signature dishes include assorted seafood with vegetables and fresh herbs steamed in parchment, seafood crepe with saffron sauce, beef tenderloin, bouillabaisse, rack of lamb, duck à l'orange, foie gras, and country-style pâté.

With just nine stools and fourteen table seats, there's always a scramble for space at **Matt's in the Market.** Here, the single arched window gives diners a bird's-eye view of the Market clock and activity on bustling Pike Place, while jazz from owner Matt Janke's own collection plays in the background. Matt's bills itself as "a seafood bar," but it is so much more, with lunchtime offerings such as catfish po' boys, muffalettas, and filé gumbo swimming with rock shrimp and andouille sausage. Dinner menus change with the seasons, but are skewed toward seafood and inspired by what Matt finds in the Market on his twice-daily shopping excursions. Matt's personal

favorites make up the wine and beer list, which comfortably matches the menu in style and price. Hearty desserts such as bread pudding or fruit crisp invite diners to linger a while and finish their meals on a sweet, homey note.

Chez Shea is another "room with a view," located just steps from Matt's. Since 1983, this romantic thirty-seat restaurant has been serving contemporary regional cuisine from its eagle's nest location on the upper level of the Corner Market building. The restaurant's towering arched windows overlook the famous neon clock, the rooftops of the Market, and the ferryboats and tankers that ply ever-active Elliott Bay. Four-course, fixed-price dinners highlight the seasonal flavors of the Pacific Northwest.

The Mediterranean-leaning offshoot of Chez Shea is located right next door. **Shea's Lounge** is a casual, chic place to sip a cocktail or glass of wine, enjoy an appetizer or three, or choose from the short list of entrées. Dishes prepared in the styles of Spain, Portugal, and Italy using fresh, locally grown ingredients change with the seasons. They might include Portuguese garlic soup, summer seafood pasta pie, Pecorino Romano flan, lemon bread pudding, and hazelnut praline Bavarian.

In the north end of the Market, diners can take advantage of several interesting views at **Avenue One.** The outside patio, fronting lively

Left: A crafts vendor packs up for the day.

FUSION FLANK STEAK

Several shops in the Market are a boon to the adventurous cook. The Souk, MarketSpice, and Oriental Mart offer large selections of unusual spices, herbs, and specialty foods from around the globe, which whip up quickly into this flavorful marinade for beef. When heated, the marinade cooks down into a thick, mellow sauce.

¼ cup seasoned rice vinegar

¼ cup mirin (Japanese rice wine) or dry sherry

2 tablespoons regular or low-sodium soy sauce

2 tablespoons sesame or peanut oil

1 tablespoon Worcestershire sauce

1 tablespoon ground coriander

1 tablespoon ground sweet paprika

1 teaspoon firmly packed palm sugar or dark brown sugar

1 teaspoon toasted sesame oil

1 teaspoon freshly grated gingerroot

½ to 1 whole fresh jalapeño pepper, rinsed, seeds and membranes removed, and diced (see note)

2 cloves garlic, thinly sliced

½ teaspoon ground allspice

¼ teaspoon ground cardamom

¼ teaspoon ground cinnamon

¼ teaspoon ground cloves

1 flank steak (1 to 1¼ pounds)

1. In a large, nonreactive bowl with a lid, mix rice vinegar, mirin, soy sauce, sesame oil, Worcestershire sauce, coriander, paprika, palm sugar, toasted sesame oil, gingerroot, jalapeño pepper, garlic, allspice, cardamom, cinnamon, and cloves until sugar is dissolved. Add flank steak, turn to coat both sides, cover, and refrigerate 10 to 12 hours. Turn steak every 4 to 6 hours.

2. Half an hour before cooking, remove meat from refrigerator. Ten minutes before cooking, preheat broiler. Lightly oil a broiler pan. Pat steak dry, reserving marinade, and place steak under broiler 3 to 4 inches from heat source. Cook steak 4 to 6 minutes per side, turning once, or until medium rare. Remove from oven, cover loosely with aluminum foil, and allow to rest 5 to 10 minutes. Meanwhile, place marinade in a small saucepan and bring to a boil. Boil for 2 to 3 minutes, remove from heat, cover, and keep warm.

3. To serve, slice steak diagonally across the grain, ¼ inch thick. Place slices on a large communal platter or individual plates. Place sauce in a small pitcher or bowl and serve at the table.

Serves 4

Note: Jalapeños vary in hotness. Test by dabbing a small piece of cut pepper on the tip of your tongue. If very hot, add only half a pepper; if mild, use a whole pepper.

First Avenue, is a pleasant place to sip one of twenty wines offered by the glass, while the main dining room features a grand mural of a 1930s Parisian street scene. The back room is dark and intimate, with an inviting fireplace and views of Puget Sound. Menu standouts include tuna tartare, shiitake mushroom salad, herb-crusted beef fillet with black olive demiglace, and chocolate pots de crème.

Jumpin' Joints

The Market is home to a wide variety of after-dark entertainment. **Patti Summers Cabaret** may be the only restaurant in Seattle where the owner is also the chef and the entertainer. Wearing so many hats would wear down most mortals, but gutsy Patti Summers has been at it since 1984, when she and her bassist and husband, Gary Steele, opted out of the lounge circuit to open their restaurant, bar, and jazz club down a shallow flight of steps at the busiest corner of the Market.

Nowadays, there's a grottolike atmosphere in the cozy, softly lit room, and not a bad seat in the house. Patti's menu leans toward the Italian, and every evening, after feeding her guests, she whips off her apron, dons her evening gown, and begins belting out old standards, joyous jazz classics, and compositions of her own.

Right: The Market is full of nooks and crannies for quiet escape from the crowds.

The **Alibi Room** is a subterranean, darkly atmospheric place just off lower Post Alley, where local actors, screenwriters, and producers hang out for stimulating conversation, a simple meal, and a glass of wine. Several well-known thespians, including Rob Morrow and Tom Skerritt, have invested in this wine bar/restaurant. Their goal is to create an environment for local independent filmmakers to talk about their craft, hold poetry readings and script read-throughs, and host quarterly film festivals.

On Friday and Saturday evenings, the portion of Post Alley just across from the Alibi Room becomes congested with Gen Xers ready to participate in **Unexpected Productions' TheatreSports** program, which bills itself as "improvisational theatre with a competitive

edge." The two-hundred-seat Market Theatre, with its low ceilings and bare colored lightbulbs, is an atmospheric venue for the ensemble cast of thirty-two improvisational actors who create scenes based entirely on audience suggestions.

Tucked under the Market Theatre sign, down a winding cobbled path along Post Alley, you'll find **Il Bistro,** which for more than twenty years has served traditional Italian cuisine in a subterranean series of vaulted rooms. With its low ceilings, dimly lit dining room, always-humming stepdown bar, and beguiling archways, Il Bistro is one of those romantic, inviting places that keep calling you back.

Cioppino, balsamic-glazed salmon, Caesar salad, and rack of lamb marinated in rosemary and garlic with sangiovese wine sauce are some of the signature dishes. The bar is worth trying in and of itself, with its knowledgeable, fun-loving bartender and wide selection of coffee drinks, single-malt Scotches, brandies, grappas, and Cognacs.

Upper Post Alley comes alive Wednesday through Saturday nights, thanks to **Kells Irish Restaurant & Pub.** A crush of people stand shoulder to shoulder at the hundred-year-old bar imported from Ireland, while a live band plays Irish music. Contented patrons talk animatedly over the sound of the music and knock back heavy mugs of Guinness Stout and Harp

Those who wish to sample the Market lifestyle on a temporary basis opt for **Pensione Nichols** or the **Inn at the Market**. The Inn, a Mobil Four Star and AAA Four Diamond award-winning boutique hotel, offers sixty-five French country–style rooms and suites with spectacular views of the Market, the cityscape, and Puget Sound. The open-air, flower-strewn fifth-floor deck is a relaxing place to enjoy summer sunsets and a glass of Northwest wine. Pensione Nichols, a bed-and-breakfast inn, boasts ten rooms with shared baths, two suites with private baths and full kitchens, and Sound views. The **American Youth Hostel**, a Market neighbor located just south of the historical district, on Post Alley, can house two hundred.

Lager. As the night progresses, the air grows heavy with cigarette smoke, and many customers sing along to traditional Irish folk songs.

This wee bit o' Ireland opened in 1983 after owners Joe and Ethna McAleese emigrated from Belfast. As patriarch Joe or another member of the McAleese clan escorts you to a table in the dark, low-ceilinged dining room, you'll feel as though you've been transported to a rustic country inn cum workingman's pub.

Left: The Market houses a variety of unique shops and galleries, which make for pleasant strolling and impulse buying.

"Julie, Julie, Julie"

Julie Cascioppo is in character as "Irene," a disgruntled poet from San Francisco, one of the many personalities she portrays at her once-a-week cabaret show at the **Pink Door.** Dressed in black from head to toe, her nails glossy red and sharp as daggers, "Irene" practically growls the words to a feminist standard from the 1970s.

"I am woman, hear me roar, in numbers too big to ignore," she belts out while a table full of tourists from Australia laugh and clap. Just in front of the stage, a group of young friends who drove in from Kent, Washington, just for the show applaud and whistle when the torch singer finishes her song.

When Julie/Irene asks if anyone in the crowd is celebrating a birthday or anniversary, a middle-aged woman raises her hand and points hesitantly toward her daughter, who is celebrating her twenty-sixth birthday with dinner and the show. Julie/Irene calls her up on stage, asks her all sorts of embarrassing questions about her personal life, then invites everyone to join in singing "Happy Birthday." It's all part of the kitschy, campy atmosphere here.

Since its opening in 1981, access to the Pink Door has been discreet and anonymous, almost like an insider's secret. Look for the pink door along Post Alley and head down a flight of steep stairs into the high-ceilinged main dining room,

the ever-popular bar, or the rooftop terrace, which is open May to September.

The patio is one of the best places in the Market, indeed in the whole city, to sit outside on a sunny summer's day. Latticework and hanging baskets dapple the faces of the young and young at heart. Ladies in straw hats mingle comfortably with youths in black leather. It's like a garden party with a hundred intriguing friends.

Inside the main dining room, a harlequin clown mural soars overhead, candles glimmer on the oilcloth-covered tables, cherub statues smile beatifically, and the fountain at the center of the

When walking near City Fish, look down at the brown tiles paving the floor. Between rows 351 and 352 you will find Nancy and Ronald Reagan's tiles, two of the 46,500 **Market tiles** installed in 1986 as part of the "Be a Legend in Your Own Tile" campaign. For just $35, you could buy a square and have it inscribed with a name or a message. Look for the tiles etched with the prime numbers from 1 to 100 in front of DeLaurenti's main entrance; they were given by the wife of a mathematician in honor of her husband.

Right: Triangle Building businesses locked up for the evening.

WILD MUSHROOM BUTTER WITH CROSTINI

In the spring and fall, Northwest forests burst into life with wild mushrooms sporting lyrical names—chanterelles, morels, hedgehogs, black trumpets. When paired with sweet butter, a touch of garlic, and a hint of Cognac, their musky flavor makes a distinctive appetizer.

½ pound fresh wild Northwest mushrooms, such as chanterelles, morels, black trumpets, hedgehogs, and/or porcini, or a mixture of several varieties

¾ cup (1½ sticks) unsalted butter, at room temperature

2 medium cloves garlic, peeled and cut into thin slices

2 teaspoons minced fresh marjoram or 1 teaspoon dried marjoram, crumbled

¼ teaspoon kosher salt

¼ teaspoon freshly ground black pepper

3 tablespoons Cognac or dry sherry (optional)

1. Wipe mushrooms with a soft-bristled brush to remove any traces of dirt or pine needles, then chop coarsely.

2. Melt ¼ cup of the butter in a medium skillet over medium-high heat, and add mushrooms and garlic. Cook 2 to 3 minutes, or until mushrooms absorb butter and begin to shrink, stirring constantly. Reduce heat to medium-low and add marjoram, salt, and pepper, stirring well. Cook 4 to 5 minutes more, or until mushrooms shrink and garlic is tender, stirring occasionally. Remove mushrooms from heat and allow to cool.

3. Place the remaining ½ cup butter in a food processor or blender and pulse briefly. Add the mushrooms, pan juices, and Cognac, and pulse until mixture is well blended but mushrooms still have a bit of texture. Taste and adjust seasonings. Scoop mushroom butter into an attractive ramekin or bowl, smooth the surface, cover, and refrigerate 1 hour or, preferably, overnight, to allow flavors to meld.

4. Remove mushroom butter from refrigerator ½ hour before serving. Prepare crostini. Place ramekin in the center of a large plate or platter and surround with crostini.

Makes 1½ cups

CROSTINI

1 narrow loaf French or Italian bread, sliced ¼ inch thick

Preheat the broiler. Arrange bread slices on a baking sheet and place 3 to 4 inches from heat source. Broil 1 to 2 minutes on each side, until golden brown. Remove from oven and serve warm or at room temperature.

The Market's best-known symbol is the world-famous **Public Market Center sign**, on the right side of which is the Market clock, which glows in vivid pink/orange neon twenty-four hours a day. It is one of the earliest pieces of neon in the city, dating from the late 1920s or early 1930s.

room gurgles good-naturedly along with the animated crowd. The food is classically Italian with an emphasis on organic Northwest produce, pastas, and seafood. Specialties of the house include lasagne Pink Door, *zuppa di pesce* (fish soup), and housemade gnocchi. Owner Jackie Roberts, also known as Jacquelina di Roberto, "La Padrona," oversees the entertaining, fun-filled atmosphere with a sense of humor and a touch of class.

They Come Out at Night

Jeff Jarvis, the Market's swing-shift facilities production supervisor, radios in his position to his coworkers. He's in the DownUnder section and it's close to I A.M. Jeff and his crew of seven, whom he fondly refers to as "stagehands," have been working since 5:30 P.M. With just another hour and a half to go, they're winding down for the night—locking up, hosing off the streets one last time, and making sure everything is clean and tidy.

The bright arcade lighting stays on twenty-four hours a day in this less-traveled part of the Market; even so, there's an eerie feeling in the DownUnder this time of the early morning. It's simply so silent down here among the heavy wood timbers and glistening wood floors.

The numerous reports of ghost sightings in the Market don't help Jeff's concentration any. Although the longtime Market employee has never encountered a specter, one evening at the stroke of midnight, a crew member did. Taking a short breather after waxing the floor, the man reportedly felt someone untuck the back of his shirt. Thinking it was a mischievous coworker, he turned quickly, but nobody was there. Or anywhere else nearby.

Princess Angeline reigns as the Market's most famous spirit. The blue-eyed Native American was the daughter of Chief Sealth, for whom Seattle is named. Angeline's restless spirit reputedly roams the corridors of the DownUnder and picks plums under cover of darkness from the haunted plum tree in the Soames-Dunn courtyard. She appears as a bright white form dressed in rags. Beware to all who spot her vivid blue eyes, however. Legend has it that a curse will be inherited by those who see her ghost.

The Economy Market is another hot spot for ghostbusters. Here the specter of a dapper gentleman still waltzes in the present-day Meeting Place, a popular venue for social events and wedding receptions as well as company meetings for Northwest corporate giants like Microsoft and Amazon.com.

During the 1920s, this area was home to the Economy Dance Hall. While in town, sailors on shore leave and other First Avenue itinerants could drop a dime for a ninety-second "taxi dance" with a pretty young "hostess." The hostess and the dance hall management split the profits. If the hostess enticed the man into buying refreshments, she got an extra commission. You can still see the sign that advertises "OLD TIME DANCE TONITE" on a heavy wooden beam above the second-story landing.

From behind a certain plate glass window in the Economy Market, the ghost of Arthur Goodwin reputedly stares down at what was once his domain—the people, cars, and buildings along bustling Pike Place. Arthur was the nephew of Frank Goodwin, the man who founded the Market.

After Frank sold his share of the Market to his protégé in 1925, Arthur ran the Market on a grand scale. He installed better lighting and planter boxes, increased advertising, and staged free vaudeville shows in the old Municipal Market

Building along Western Avenue. He built himself a mahogany-paneled office with a huge conference table, tiled fireplace, and sweeping view. It's the location of the present-day Goodwin Library and the site of Arthur's hauntings.

Sadly, the Depression cut short Arthur's grandiose plans. The vaudeville performers played their last act and Arthur barely spent enough money to make routine repairs to the Market's buildings. In time, he lost control of his fiefdom. Perhaps that's why his ghost broods behind glass today, wondering how things might have been.

Tomorrow Is Another Day

By 4 A.M., the compost has been recycled, the garbage picked up, and the 46,500 tiles lining the Main and North Arcades have been hosed off and dried. Reflections from the rows of bright lights in the Main Arcade bounce off the hard, utilitarian surfaces designed so long ago by Frank Goodwin to showcase the produce and product, not the architecture.

At this early hour, few souls are in sight. But it won't be long before the energetic hordes descend on these history-packed halls. As it has done since its inception on August 17, 1907, the Pike Place Market awaits the dawn of another day.

Left: Last light projects the Public Market sign onto the Triangle Building.

RECIPE LIST